"In *Your Pain Has a Name*, Monica DiCristina skillfully and compassionately invites us to honor the truths of our lives and stories. In doing so, she guides us toward one of the greatest paradoxes of all: Turning toward our pain helps us find a way through it. This book is a tender and winsome resource for healing."

—Aundi Kolber, MA, LPC, therapist and author
of *Try Softer* and *Strong Like Water*

"*Your Pain Has a Name* is oxygen, fuel, and companionship for the journey of self-acceptance and inner peace many humans find inaccessible. In a stunningly vulnerable way, Monica DiCristina walks alongside us, inviting us to investigate our past stories and build new, healthier paths forward. With her uncanny ability to convey difficult concepts through simple, relatable examples, Monica offers liberation from the false narratives that limit our ability to live life to the fullest. This book is a gift of love."

el Macy Stafford, *New York Times*
lling author of *Hands Free Mama*,
Only Love Today, and *Soul Shift*

"Our worth is often a treasure buried. Monica gets to excavating the truth: Our worth was always there, and our pain was telling us a different story. In *Your Pain Has a Name*, Monica takes us through the fog and smoke of our pain to return to ourselves, the true story, the value we have always had. From her time-tested experience and compassion-held knowledge, you will find the wealth of your worth here."

—J. S. Park, hospital chaplain and author of
As Long As You Need: Permission to Grieve

"We have all lived different stories that shape our particular feelings about our identity and sense of safety. But many of us have never considered that our wounds have specific names or know where to start when it comes to untangling our stories. For anyone looking for a compassionate guide to understanding your story and for anyone that feels ready to rewrite the narratives that cause harm to your relationship with yourself and others, this book is your first step! I cherish Monica's voice in my life and always look forward to reading her soulful words. I know you will feel the same as you read the impactful message on these pages!"

—Nicole Zasowski, licensed marriage and family therapist, author of *What If It's Wonderful?*

"Fellow therapist Monica DiCristina has written a must-read guide for anyone seeking to learn valuable tools [in order] to thrive following unnamed emotional pain, anxiety, and trauma. Monica continues to bring her unique voice, personal stories, and insights, and a commitment to help others through *Your Pain Has a Name*. This book is a raw and remarkable call not only to heal ourselves but also to begin to think about mental health support and healing in a broader way."

—Chinwé Williams, PhD, LPC, therapist and coauthor of *Seen: Healing Despair and Anxiety in Kids and Teens Through the Power of Connection*

"In *Your Pain Has a Name*, Monica DiCristina becomes a gentle companion to weary hearts, offering calm, comfort, and compassion. Her storytelling is approachable and wise—affirming our pain while leading us toward wholeness. Drawing on her years as a therapist, Monica puts words to the deep hurts we carry and guides us on a path toward healing. If you're wondering if this book is for you...it is."

—Kayla Craig, author *Every Season Sacred* and *To Light Their Way*, creator of Liturgies for Parents

"In *Your Pain Has a Name*, Monica DiCristina is more than an author and purveyor of words on pages. She is a gentle and profoundly knowledgeable guide who invites us into the sacred practice of seeing the truth about ourselves. The truth that is too often overshadowed and distorted because of past and present pain. From the first page to the last, we are met with compassion and empathy, alongside accessible and practical tools to apply to our journey of rediscovering our truest selves. Monica has done a beautiful job of providing us with the safety and comfort to explore our own redemption stories, as we are empowered to name our pain and heal."

—Patricia A. Taylor, writer and anti-racism educator

"To over-identify with one's hurts or traumas can trap us. To deny being hurt can leave us divided. Meanwhile, navigating life as a person with injuries, scars, and wounds is essential to being wholly human. Thank God for Monica DiCristina. With *Your Pain Has a Name*. Monica continues the essential work she's been doing for years, helping you and I avoid the extremes of emotional indulgence and denial, and moving us to what might best be described as as 'health.'"

—Justin McRoberts, author of *Sacred Strides: The Journey to Belovedness in Work and Rest*

"In *Your Pain Has a Name: A Therapist's Invitation to Understanding Your Story and Sorting Out Who You Are from What Hurts*, Monica DiCristina writes from a deep well of healing brilliance both from a therapist's perspective and as someone who has had to name her own pain. This book is not about quick fixes or theory-heavy techniques; rather, it focuses on the forgotten art of presence, using safe space as a catalyst for naming pain or understanding unnamed pain. As she explains, 'Unnamed pain, which swirls around inside without understanding, definition, or boundaries, can tell stories about who you are. These stories are often harsh and untrue.' This book is for therapists, people just starting therapy, those who have yet to process and name their pain, and anyone genuinely seeking a journey of healing and, as DiCristina says, as many guides have stated, 'coming home to yourself.' I chose to endorse this book because it is real, and I believe it will comfort and meet people in the reality of their pain—especially the unnamed pain."

—Dr. Terence Lester, founder of Love
Beyond Walls and author of *I See You*,
When We Stand, and *All God's Children*

"Prepare to be transformed. Each page of Monica's book *Your Pain Has a Name* is a profound gift of honesty, compassion, and soul-deep wisdom. Monica has a remarkable way of gently inviting us to face our pain with intention and courage. Through her words, both in this book and beyond—whether on social media, her podcast, or her other works—Monica offers us the tools to rewrite our stories and forge a future that heals life's deepest wounds. She teaches us to approach healing with both curiosity and grace, making this one of the most affirming and essential reads of our time."

—Tasha Hunter, MSW, LCSW,
author of *Liberation, Tell Me Where It Hurts*,
and *What Children Remember*

"Opening the door to her 15-year therapy practice, Monica has invited readers to come and take a seat beside her. With a deeply humanizing tenderness, her words are a trustworthy companion. Her untangling of overly used words such as *trauma, gaslighting*, and *boundaries* is worth the price of the book alone. Luckily for the reader, there's so much more here—a healing balm for anyone seeking solace."

—Marcie Alvis Walker, author of
Everybody Come Alive: A Memoir in Essays

"Provocative and enlightening. Monica DiCristina skillfully takes us into some of the therapeutic dark places of our pain and not only shines a helpful light on where it originates, where it is perpetuated and can be changed, but also illuminates the hindrances and 'pretenders of helpfulness' to avoid in our journeys toward healing. A great resource for beginning the process of naming and changing."

—Terry Hargrave PhD and Sharon
Hargrave, MA, founders of Restoration
Therapy and authors of *Five Days to a New Self*

Monica DiCristina

YOUR PAIN HAS A NAME

A Therapist's Invitation to Understanding Your Story and Sorting Out Who You Are from What Hurts

WORTHY
— PUBLISHING —

Nashville • New York

Worthy

Hachette Book Group

1290 Avenue of the Americas, New York, NY 10104

worthypublishing.com

@WorthyPub

First Edition: May 2025

Worthy is a division of Hachette Book Group, Inc. The Worthy name and logo are registered trademarks of Hachette Book Group, Inc.

The publisher is not responsible for websites (or their content) that are not owned by the publisher.

The Hachette Speakers Bureau provides a wide range of authors for speaking events. To find out more, go to hachettespeakersbureau .com or email HachetteSpeakers@hbgusa.com.

Worthy Books may be purchased in bulk for business, educational, or promotional use. For information, please contact your local bookseller or the Hachette Book Group Special Markets Department at special.markets@hbgusa.com.

Print book interior design by Amy Quinn

Library of Congress Cataloging-in-Publication Data

Names: DiCristina, Monica, author.

Title: Your pain has a name : a therapist's invitation to understanding your story and sorting out who you are from what hurts / Monica DiCristina.

Description: First edition. | Nashville : Worthy, 2025.

Identifiers: LCCN 2024053649 | ISBN 9781546006428 (trade paperback) | ISBN 9781546006435 (ebook)

Subjects: LCSH: Self-acceptance. | Self-actualization (Psychology) | Psychic trauma.

Classification: LCC BF575.S37 D49 2025 | DDC 158.1—dc23/eng/20250212

LC record available at https://lccn.loc.gov/2024053649

ISBNs: 9781546006428 (trade paperback), 9781546006435 (ebook)

Printed in the United States of America

LSC-C

Printing 1, 2025

To anyone who has felt alone in their unnamed pain

CONTENTS

Contents

Dear Reader,

As a younger therapist, I had a client in my care who had experienced a devastating loss. Feeling like I was in over my head, I called a more seasoned therapist, hoping to find the secret code to solve her pain. The older therapist assured me that there was no code, no shortcut, no simple solution to the woman's pain. Or to anyone's pain, for that matter. "You already have what you need to give her," he said. "What she needs now is your presence."

What I learned is that, in the absence of quick fixes, there is the grounding companionship of being *with* someone in their pain.

I hope to be with you in this book.

Your pain may be all-consuming like my client's, or it may be the daily irritation of a life that doesn't fit you, or something in between. Pain doesn't discriminate, and it doesn't follow the rules we've tried to set for it.

Pain demands our attention for it to be settled, soothed, and understood.

In the absence of being able to eliminate anyone's pain as a therapist, I have found that instead I offer them my presence, helping them to find understanding and in that understanding, relief.

I became a therapist in the hope of helping people become free to be who they were created to be. In the process, though, I encountered a daunting adversary, one I know well myself—unnamed pain. Unnamed pain, which swirls around inside without understanding, definition, or boundaries, can tell stories about who you are. These stories are often harsh and untrue.

In order to help people have compassion for, know, and love themselves, I have to help them learn to understand their pain—and to name it.

Because if you don't name your pain, it will name you.

The first step to knowing and loving yourself is understanding what has kept you from that knowledge.

This process can be comforting, like folding yourself into a soft blanket. It can be soothing, like a warm cup of tea cradled in your tired hands. It can also be fierce, like charging into battle to reclaim who you are. It can be steady, like holding the hand of the child you once were. And it can be grievous, like a sudden burst of tears you've been holding as you held your breath all these years.

What I have found in each of these experiences is relief—the relief that comes with understanding.

Whatever the process holds for *you*, my hope is that you won't feel alone, and that in finding names for your pain, you will find the way to come home to yourself.

Dear Reader

This book is me putting my hand in yours, and saying, "Let's look at this together." I'm rooting for you. I care about you even though I've never met you. I'm thinking of you as I write, and I hope you hear the love and care in these words from me to you.

With you,
Monica

INTRODUCTION

When first-time clients come into my office, they usually don't feel great, but they often don't know why.

Can you relate?

Sometimes they come through my door, wanting to understand themselves more, maybe to work on a new relationship or to repair an old one. Something feels off, perhaps, or something has happened, or something hurts so badly it demands their attention.

Regardless, we start with what hurts, which is usually the best place to start.

The lighting in my office is intentionally soft, the colors muted and blended. The sunlight streams through the wall of windows. The art is simple, the shelves uncluttered. The sound machine hums from the hallway, surrounding us and blocking noise from the outside world. I quietly close the door.

The aim is not to achieve an aesthetic style but rather to ease the awkwardness of the first visit for a client, creating a welcoming environment and a place they feel comfortable returning to.

It's hard to walk into a therapist's office for the first time. I know; I've done it. You scan the walls, the therapist. You wonder if this will help or be a letdown. You wonder if there is any way to understand what you are grappling with. You wonder if the therapist will even understand. You wonder if the therapist will be strange. Or worse, you wonder if the therapist will think *you* are strange.

There are few things more vulnerable than telling someone you just met what hurts, trying to explain what's wrong, what's not working, and dealing with the anxious anticipation of questions, prying into your past. That kind of baring of the soul is a lot to expect from another human being. So I tell my clients that this is a safe and sacred space, that what they say in here is confidential. Then I tell them to just start anywhere. We fumble our way through the awkwardness of first conversations, then we begin to explore what is really going on.

I see it like landing a plane. We are circling the runway. It's normal to go slowly. As the emotional safety of the conversation progresses, the plane begins its descent.

I'll be honest: Even after all these years, there are moments when I wonder if the plane will land. Will this person feel safe enough to become vulnerable? But as the plane begins to get closer to the ground, we get closer to the pain.

Sometimes the landing is smooth, other times it is

bumpy, when clients are surprised by how much they feel. Here, the plane lands, flying under the superficial elevation at which the person has to fly in the rest of their life. Here, we land on what hurts, what's not working, what's not on the cheerful holiday card.

Here, we find pain. Along the way, we find an invitation to understand the pain, or at least bring some measure of comfort.

Pain is an invitation to find names for your pain, which is the first step to returning home to who you were made to be.

And yet nobody wants to talk about pain. It seems counterintuitive to start there, doesn't it? But everyone who enters my office comes with pain they don't understand. Everyone shows up not feeling good in some way and wanting something to be different.

We start there.

We start with how that hurt has confused you. If you don't, you will never find your way to the truth of who you are.

The process may seem daunting, but it is not to be feared but rather to be embraced.

Imagine, for example, a hurting child running to you with a skinned knee and bleeding elbow, crying. You wouldn't shoo the kid away, would you? Or give her a lecture on how her crying is too much and too loud. You wouldn't point out that she hasn't learned how to tie her shoes (like her classmates), and that she's about to trip on them again. You wouldn't shame her for being hurt or tell her to grow up.

You would bend down and say something like, "What hurts?"

You deserve this same tenderness.

We can't avoid pain, but we can learn to face it instead of fleeing from it. And we can get incredibly precise by learning to accurately identify and validate what we feel. Language is essential in this. This is a lot of what this book is about.

We are here to find the language for your pain so you can understand it better. This includes letting your language be as complex as needed in order to be truthful. With this understanding comes more freedom. And that freedom comes by separating yourself from the narratives of your pain.

Naming your pain is a posture of leaning in to listen to yourself and to your story. So give it the space to speak. If you don't, your story will become minimized to the point that it can easily be dismissed, not only in the distant past but in the day-to-day present.

Recognize that a name is not necessarily a diagnosis. This is not a book of diagnoses. Diagnoses can be very helpful, necessary even, for relief. But I don't believe that self-diagnosing a clinical condition in a book is a sound, therapeutic practice. If you are looking for a diagnosis, I suggest you find the caring presence of a skilled professional. Don't give up. This book may be one stepping stone forward on that important path.

Even in capable hands, not every hurt can be healed. Every hurt, though, can be honored. We honor it by seeing it and naming it. In doing that, we unearth who we are from underneath the rubble of what hurts. And we see, possibly for the first time, a glint of the untarnished self that has been there all along.

It is going into the pain that allows you to bring your true self into the light.

In the course of this book, I will walk you through the ruins of what I have lived, along with the stories of others. Each of us learned how to name our own particular pain. And all of us found our way home. We took different roads to get there, but we got there.

My work is grounded in science. But in my experience, I have found that the practice of therapy is more an art than a science. The fact that it is less clinical and more creative is why story is so essential. That is why I use so many of them. It is also why *you* are so essential. You are the best witness to the story you have lived.

A note on stories in this book: The only story without alterations is my own. The other stories are more like allegories from fifteen years of working with clients. The details have been obscured in order to anonymize them. The stories are not factual accounts. Although I refer to one person at a time, I am referring to many. There are common themes I see in my work, and these stories represent a combination of those, not individual lives.

This book is divided into three parts, charting the journey we will travel together.

Part 1: The Problem—Living with Unnamed Pain

This section focuses on some of the reasons we find ourselves living with unnamed pain. I will share my own story and the stories of others, trying to find understanding—often without much success. This can be big experiences, like the wrong diagnosis, or daily experiences, like running into invalidation. Learning to listen to yourself is the way to cross the bridge into the journey to understanding your own pain and therefore your own story.

Part 2: The Journey—Finding Names for Your Pain

In this section, I share how, in discovering names for my pain, I developed a passion for helping others do the same. We will dig into specific types of pain and equip you with tools to excavate your own story. This section includes learning how to look for clues, how to cope with sometimes overwhelming feelings in naming your pain, how pains from the past intrude on the present, along with the impact of present-day pains. This section concludes with a new compassionate understanding for how we have learned to cope.

Part 3: The Returning—You Are Not Your Pain

In Part 3, we come home. Your increased understanding has cleared away so much rubble that it will reunite you with the person who has always been under that pile of pain. We will explore how you are, in fact, *not* your pain. This section is about separating who you are from your narratives and the erroneous conclusions you may have drawn from them, freeing you so you can come home to your true self.

This is finding a more accurate understanding of who you are. We will explore how to take this idea of starting where it hurts in order to understand your story, your day, and what you need next.

Additional resources curated on my website (monica dicristina.com) will allow you to explore topics in this book in greater depth. Each chapter has its own list. There will be more information (books and links) about specific pains, diagnoses, traumas, and grief to support you on your naming journey. And since this book addresses emotional pain rather than physical pain, you will find books about physical pain there, too. The library holds works by researchers I look to, as well as diverse voices so that, hopefully, you can find one that reflects more of your individual experience.

This book is a homecoming, a loving reunion with who you are. You are invited. Your pain, anger, frustration, your shame, every hurting part of you is welcome here. They all are great places to start your journey.

You don't have to have it mapped out or figured out. You are not a project to be fixed or a problem to be managed; you are a beautiful creation. We're going to do this book differently than maybe you have done with others. We are going to engage with this book from a less pressured posture. So go ahead, lower your shoulders and exhale. Put down your highlighters (unless you love them) and abandon all your "shoulds."

Just be here, that's all. That's the invitation. There's hope here, but no pressure. There's no deadline for this journey, so there's no rush. We naturally want things to go fast, especially when we are hurting. But faster is not always better.

Start where you are, with where it hurts, which is the most compassionate place to begin. Together we will get there, no matter how long it takes.

So let's start here with *What is hurting?*

PART 1

THE PROBLEM–
LIVING WITH UNNAMED PAIN

CHAPTER 1

STUCK IN THE WRONG STORY

"I am out with lanterns, looking for myself."

EMILY DICKINSON

I have rewritten this chapter six times now. There was too much of my story. Not enough of it. Or too much of it, too soon. It was exhausting.

The irony of having to rehash my story is not lost on me. Besides the fact that as a therapist I don't normally share this information, I never wanted to tell it in the first place. I never wanted *you*, the reader, to know about it. Or anyone else, for that matter. Why? Because it felt like a secret I had to hide. I shuddered when I was younger to think of anyone finding out about it, fearing what might happen. I thought it would disqualify me from society, from being close to people, from being fully known.

I worked really hard *not* to tell my story or share my fears and my terrifying thoughts. To anyone. For years, actually.

That is, until I couldn't hold them in anymore, and they came spilling out everywhere, to anyone who seemed like they might be able to help. Did it help, all this telling of my secrets? Honestly? Not really. Because no one had any idea what to do with the information, or with me.

But before we go any further, let me tell you what I know now as a practicing therapist. I am sharing this vulnerable story here in service to what I believe to be true: Not understanding our pain will amplify, prolong, and isolate us in our struggles. And we then confuse ourselves with our pain. You will see that in my story, and I see it in the unique stories I sit with.

So, like reading the ending of a book first, here are the names for my pain. Then I will walk you through what it was like to live for years without this relief and understanding. My story isn't one of hardship. It is a legacy of the echoing silence of unnamed pain and the narratives we construct to fill that gaping silent space.

I experienced sexual violations in my younger years,

early experiences that set into motion a deep lack of trust in myself and an even deeper shame. It happened at a time developmentally when kids think they are omnipotent. Believing it was all my fault, I was sure I was bad. Without understanding this common response to early trauma, I continued to fill in the story of *why* I felt so bad.

I carried this shame and unprocessed trauma into my adolescence, and during those years, I learned about some historical traumas in my family, and that someone we knew had been abusive. That's when I imploded. I began to fear that if this person we knew could do something that bad, then I might be worse than I'd feared. This new information latched onto the pain from my early traumas, and my shame produced terrifying new narratives.

Before this discovery, I had been afraid of childish things, like I was a vampire but didn't know it. But now my fears had grown too big, and I felt I couldn't talk about any of them. The cocktail of unresolved trauma, my paralyzing shame, a legacy of silent pain, and a lack of self-trust ushered in the roar of an anxiety disorder that began to take over my inner world.

I had an intense onset of undiagnosed obsessive-compulsive disorder (onset for OCD is usually between late childhood and early adulthood; it is estimated about one in one hundred people have it, and most go four-teen to seventeen years without a diagnosis).[1] I would later find out the name for the symptom of OCD I was experiencing during adolescence is ego-dystonic intrusive thoughts. These are unwanted, scary thoughts that can be violent, sexual, terrifying, and very upsetting. It is like living in a horror movie when these thoughts start to play through your mind. Imagine the worst thought that has ever popped into your mind, the most terrifying and disturbing one. And then imagine it never goes away, but instead repeats on a loop and grows limbs, sprouting new variations without ending. This can be part of other mental health diagnoses, like perinatal obsessive-compulsive disorder, when new moms have terrifying unwanted thoughts of hurting their babies or of harm coming to their child. I had thoughts just as upsetting as a teen all the way through college. People don't talk about this very often because it's embarrassing, and the disclosure alone can feel so shameful. People who struggle with these thoughts don't want them, and they go against their character. But until they know that the thoughts are OCD, they think they *are* them. I certainly did. And when you are inundated with these thoughts constantly, you also begin to doubt who you are. My sense of self-trust, already fragile from the early traumas, was shattered.

But I didn't know *any* of this then.

I just knew that the pain I was experiencing was unbearable, and I couldn't keep living with it. Without an accurate understanding of my struggles, I concluded I was indeed as bad as I feared. I got to the point of pondering suicide because I just wanted it to stop. I just wanted not to feel so bad. I looked around for anything or anyone to help.

At the height of my mental health struggles in the late nineties, I also became a Christian. I was in and out of a lot of churches back then, churches that leaned heavily on the power of prayer as the solution for human ailments. There was a lot of Bible and not a lot of anything else. So there I was, a vortex of terrifying and sometimes violent thoughts swirling around in my head, fearful of myself, but desperate for help. But when I did share, some people stared back in shock, confusion, or even fear. Now, to be fair, many were kind, even compassionate, but they were completely uninformed, maybe even weirded out.

The first big tell I did was at sixteen to a poor unsuspecting pastor of a suburban church in Georgia. We didn't go to church much as a family. But I was desperate. I ran to the altar many times to be "healed" of my scary thoughts, not only at this church but at countless others in the years that followed.

When I sat in this pastor's office, he made sure the door was open so the female secretary could be nearby—a precaution, I guess, for talking alone with a teenage girl. When I began to tell him my fears, he quickly shushed me. I am sure now that he was just trying to protect me, but that shush at the mere mention of my struggles felt like shame running through my body. Afterward, I walked alone to my little car in the almost empty parking lot, as the last couple of lights in the church lobby turned off. It would be one of many walks I took alone after unsuccessfully looking for help.

He had no idea what was wrong with me.

Neither did I.

Up to that point I had suffered for years with those disturbing images flashing through my mind. Terrified, I would, metaphorically and sometimes literally, hold my breath in an attempt to will those images never to return. Well, you know what they say about thoughts you try not to have—you have them.

I was anxious all the time. When the anxiety became extreme, I sometimes had to run to the bathroom to throw up. I was so scared, so confused. I was sure no one had ever experienced this. All I wanted was to just be like everyone else.

It was absolutely humiliating in those early years of being a Christian to go up to group after group, person after person, and "confess" that I had scary thoughts. Sometimes in an attempt to find relief, I would tell them about a specific fear I had. Today, I feel so much compassion for that young version of myself. I wore the false shame like a name tag, introducing myself with it in desperation to find relief. I often wonder what those people think today. I always wondered what they thought back then. Telling so many people felt as if it would help. It never did. Why? Because no one knew what was wrong. And because they didn't, I continued to conclude something deeply disturbing must be wrong *with me*. I carried that shame, a cousin of earlier shame, with me for years. *Years.*

Do you know what it's like to live the majority of your developing years believing something is seriously wrong with you? Maybe you do. It deeply impacted me. Perhaps it has deeply impacted you, too. It was distracting, to say the least. I struggled just to keep my head above water, all the while trying to act as if I were living a normal life.

Everything looked normal on the outside. I had two hardworking parents who tried their best to care for me. Eventually, I told them about my anxiety, shame (I didn't have that word for it back then), and scary thoughts. They cared, but they didn't know what to do. It was a different time back then, and parents of my generation didn't have the awareness about mental health concerns we have today. I had an older brother I occasionally fought with but also loved and thought was the funniest person I had ever met. I played soccer, made good grades. You get the picture. No one would suspect, or even have reason to assume, that underneath all of that, I was drowning in a pool of shame. No one understood how bad the intrusive thoughts had gotten, the ones I confessed to all those poor church people.

When my mom told me about that person we knew who had been abusive, it knocked me off my axis. My adolescent brain didn't know how to process this awful news. That is when the scariest thoughts began to happen. If *someone I knew* could do *that*, what could *I* do? What did it mean? How do I make sense of it? Again, no one knew I was mentally caving, and so I never got help. And again, I concluded that something was deeply wrong with me.

Years passed.

From all outward appearances, I continued to pass for doing okay, though I had to maintain a white-knuckled grip on every moment just to do normal things. Other girls would fall asleep at sleepovers, for example, but I would be awake, racked with anxiety. While other kids my age went off to college seeming carefree and filled with hope for their futures, I went to college feeling as though I might actually die from the anxiety and the fear that filled my daily life.

These feelings became all-consuming. I still tried to get help from different faith sources, but none of them—not one—helped. Do you know what it feels like to go from person to person, from prayer meeting to Bible study, feeling like a serial killer in disguise?

It's awful.

It wasn't until my early twenties that I finally found someone who could help. My brilliant college friend said her dad was a psychologist. She seemed genuinely perplexed about what I would have to talk to him about. I thought at the time: *My God, if she only knew.*

I was so scared to see him.

But I was more scared *not* to.

I knew I couldn't live like this anymore. My mind flashed back to a lonely walk I had taken to my dorm room, whispering "help" under my breath, wondering if taking my life was the only way out of this suffering.

I showed up to see Dr. Barnes, the father of my friend, in the outdated basement of a Baptist church in Charlotte, North Carolina. I didn't know a psychologist could work in a Baptist church, much less in the basement of one. I wasn't raised in this kind of church and didn't know anything about psychology, so this was a lot to process.

He was calm, kind, and unshocked by the terrifying thoughts I spilled out all over his mahogany office. I told him the scary thoughts that assaulted me.

He listened. He told me that thoughts are just thoughts. I told him what had happened to me as a little girl, how it was all my fault. He told me it *wasn't* my fault. I told him that I was afraid I was bad, like really bad, on the inside. He told me I *wasn't*. And then he taught me about anxiety and shame.

You see, it turned out I couldn't be healed by the impassioned prayers of well-intentioned church people. It turned out that my parents, despite their great talks about worrying, couldn't help, either.

Nothing could solve it except having the right *names* for my pain. Learning what I was experiencing was *the* thing that changed everything.

Everything began to change for me in my visits with Dr. Barnes. I learned that there was nothing, in fact, wrong with me. I just hadn't yet found the names for my pain. In the absence of accurate names, I was left to the narratives my pain had whispered to me: *You are bad, there is something wrong with you—if only they knew.*

I have Dr. Barnes and, truthfully, my unnamed pain and sense of shame to thank for my career. I didn't want anyone else to feel so alone and confused about what they were feeling, so I decided to do exactly what Dr.

Barnes had done—I became a therapist. I never wanted anyone to be stuck, unable to truly become themselves because they were stuck the way I had been.

Instead of running away from what hurt me, I began running toward it, in the hope of not only finding freedom for myself but helping others find their freedom. That has become my posture not only in my personal life but also in my professional life.

I have been a practicing therapist for more than fifteen years now. I have been trained in different therapy modalities and have taken countless continuing education courses. I am always reading books in my field, mostly from researchers but also from the plethora of brilliant thinkers in this space. Like all good therapists I know, I am constantly learning. Some of the theories and approaches I have studied could not be more different. But their knowledge, though different, is invaluable. This knowledge changes and, I believe, *saves lives*.

Do you know what the one theme I see repeated in these books and theories?

Giving a name to our pain.

Maybe the name is trauma, maybe it's shame, maybe it's addicted parents, or emotionally immature ones, maybe it's codependency, maybe it's bigotry, maybe it's grief, or maybe it's a mental health diagnosis. It could be anything. And it could, at the same time, be many things. What all this knowledge has in common, regardless of the source, is that it helps us find names for painful experiences. It is in finding that name that we are able to finally understand ourselves and to find ourselves, perhaps for the first time.

When we finally flip on that light, we can see what is happening inside us. That's what all good therapy work does. It doesn't eliminate pain, it can't fix your parents, let alone the world, but it does define the hurt so that we aren't endlessly searching, even allowing it to increase. We can set boundaries between it and who we are. Pain when well defined usually becomes less overwhelming, allowing you to learn what you need to cope. And in finding the language to clearly identify that pain, *we can also find ourselves again.*

I can't say I am glad for the suffering I experienced during those years of unnamed pain. But I *can* tell you this: Finding a name for, and an understanding of, the pain you are experiencing is liberating.

I prayed for years to be free of my anxieties, free of those scary thoughts, free of feeling I was so bad. I hoped it would all just go away. *That* was the answer I was seeking. Although I can't tell you I wouldn't have welcomed that miracle, it is not what happened.

When I found, and continued to find, names for my pain, I found my freedom. I'm okay now, and I have been for a very long time. When I understood more about my anxiety, scary thoughts weren't so scary anymore. When my severe anxiety and OCD resolved, and I stopped fearing them so much, they went away. I have worked through my early traumas, naming those accurately, too. It's been more than twenty years now of relief. At times, I still struggle with random shame, and I still get anxious. I think most of us do. But now I know the name for that, too, for which I have choices.

I never got my miracle. But I got *my* name back, *after* I found names for my pain.

I am glad I didn't stop until I finally found the right help. I want to help you learn to do the same.

Let's begin with why our pains often go unnamed, as well as some of the wrong roads we sometimes find ourselves on when looking for the right names.

CHAPTER 2

THE WRONG DIAGNOSIS

"It's hard to treat what you can't—or won't—name."
MAGGIE SMITH

My youngest daughter once thought she was in a dream while she was awake. It's funny now, but at the time it was really scary for her. It turns out that, because we had been out of the country for an extended period of time in a significantly different time zone, she had jet lag.

The term meant nothing to her, not until she understood what jet lag was and what its effects were. She felt strange, tired, and groggy during the day in a way she had never experienced. Without the right diagnosis (and with the mind of a young child), she thought she was stuck in a dream she couldn't get out of. With the correct understanding, though, she was able to understand her experience.

This example illustrates an important truth: When you have the wrong diagnosis, label, or understanding for what's happening to you, it can have significant ramifications. It's pretty scary to feel stuck in a dream. Jet lag, not so much.

Why is it hard for so many of us to find names for our pain? Sometimes people come into my office after having talked to everyone they know, yet they still feel awful. You may say, well, not everyone knows therapy stuff. True, but it's more than that. It is a combination of the invalidation we are met with and the inaccurate labels we are left with.

Let's start there. When we reach out to others for help, we often either get turned away or turned around. We leave their presence, feeling either dismissed or disoriented. Why do the people we turn to for help so often do this? I think it's because most people simply don't know what to do with us when we're hurting. When we look for help from others, we often find ourselves met with oversimplification and a rush to certainty.

That can come from a person in a helping profession or from someone who just seems to know a lot. (We all have one of those in our lives.) A little knowledge is a dangerous thing, especially in the hands of those who are convinced they are always right.

Often shortsighted, sometimes long-winded, these "helpers" only see what they know how to see. Their lens is clouded by their own limitations and biases. Instead of their presence being a warm and inviting space, it is an empty hall, without empathy or answers. Left to ourselves, we often blame ourselves. "Something is wrong with me. I'm hurting, no one seems to know why, it *must* be me."

Sound familiar?

Let's say you have shoulder pain. The chiropractor sees a need for an adjustment. The physical therapist says you've got to stretch. The acupuncturist applies her needles. The orthopedist gives you a cortisone shot. Your grandma prays. And your brother-in-law tells you all about his new supplements. Each "practitioner" sees what they know how to see. None of this is necessarily wrong; it's just incomplete.

Maybe they are all *partially* right. Maybe only one of them is right. Maybe all of them are wrong. Whatever the case, we must let our pains be as complex as they need to be in order to find accurate names for them. It may not be a simple answer. Allowing the complexity to remain will help you decipher which voices to listen to.

For instance, I had a new client walk into my office once with a "work concern." When she discovered the possibility of her having autism, she left my office deeply relieved at finally understanding herself and, as a result, *loving herself more*. How did this happen? I didn't diagnose her with autism; it is out of my expertise. But I refused to let her pain be limited to the initial concern and stayed curious with her. There seemed to be more to the story.

I only saw her for a short period of time, but together we approached her concerns like a group project. We listened to the wisdom of her self-reflections, then agreed that a referral for testing was the next step. She came back to confirm the diagnosis, and she left my office with a new understanding, leading her to more clarity and love for herself.

I have had countless clients walk in with depressive symptoms and walk out with a new understanding of an autoimmune disease, a vitamin deficiency, or a hormonal imbalance. Did I diagnose them? Again, no. But I did help them find someone who could. The catalyst for the referral was our mutual engagement, ending in a shared refusal to oversimplify their pain, which would likely misdiagnose what caused it. We allowed the answer to be complex if necessary.

Many a mom sits on my sofa and tells me she has

an "irritability issue." We discover together that what she has instead is an "overwhelm issue." She is so overwhelmed that she is irritable with the very children she works so hard to care for. If we had wagged an accusatory finger at her irritability, we would never have gotten to the heart of what her real pain was.

Think about it like this. You have heard that a hammer sees everything as a nail, right? Maybe your friend just read a fantastic book on gratitude. It was life changing! The only problem is that now she is trying to change *your* life and everyone else's with her gratitude insights. Your mom refusing to respect your boundaries by coming over unannounced is now labeled by your friend as *your* "lack of gratitude for her."

You see where I am going with this?

We see what we know how to see. We also see what we want to see. Those limitations keep us from finding what we need, both in professional settings and in personal relationships.

This can feel overwhelming. And so it is important to pause here and remind ourselves that there are correct diagnoses to be found. Understanding *does* exist! Just maybe not in the prepackaged form you have been offered. The key difference is to resist the pressure to oversimplify your pain to a quick answer. Complexity is not a liability, it is an important door to finding what you need. If it doesn't feel right, keep looking. Sometimes it can feel scary to keep looking, especially if you admired or very much respected the person who wasn't able to help. People may have confidence in their diagnosis of you, but your confidence is more important. Sometimes it takes moving from a place that didn't help to another option.

Looking for Answers in All the Wrong Places

I can still feel the crunch under my feet as my college roommate and I walked across the gravel parking lot of the church we were attending, which was temporarily housed in a trailer. We walked up the wooden steps and pulled open the creaky door, looking for the pastor who had agreed to meet with us. We found him in his cramped office and sat down.

In those years I was searching and praying for help from church people. My roommate, one of the few people I had told about the thoughts that haunted me, convinced me to talk with yet *another pastor.*

The theology of two desperate kids was questionable, but my friend's love for me was not. She wanted to relieve my suffering and find an answer. And so she took me to the place she thought was trustworthy. She was a true friend.

She believed that my intrusive thoughts were spiritual

in origin. (Yes, that's how little information we had back then about mental health.) She pitched this idea to the pastor as I sat beside her in humiliation. I wanted to crawl under the ugly indoor/outdoor carpet. Unnamed pain can sometimes feel humiliating.

The pastor listened, or at least gave the appearance of listening. Without so much as a pause for reflection, he launched into a sermon about how this *couldn't* be spiritual. Those thoughts were *definitely* my own. As he condemned me to sole ownership of this problem, he looked self-satisfied. When we asked questions, he smugly dismissed them. He didn't once ask if I was okay. He didn't ask if I needed help. And just like that, we were back in the parking lot beside my friend's car, feet crunching deeper into the gravel from the weight of the added shame I was carrying.

We'd gone for help; we got a sermon. We were two college students so in need that we had driven thirty minutes to meet him, at his place, and he didn't take a minute to mention anything about mental health. He didn't suggest therapy or seeing a psychiatrist. Maybe he didn't believe in mental health care? I don't know. Whatever the case, he made his pronouncements without seeing, *really* seeing, the hurting young person sitting right in front of him.

From my years of experience as a therapist, this isn't

an isolated story. Versions of this story happen to so many people in so many different settings. I hear these stories every week.

Sometimes, people in positions of power don't wonder enough. They don't listen enough. They don't refer enough. They don't say, "I don't know, but I will help you find someone who does" enough. They don't say, "I believe you" enough. They don't say, "I'm listening" enough.

If that has been your experience, I hope you will listen to and believe your story and keep looking for the right help. It *does* exist. Find someone who will refer you, believe you, and listen to you. And I say this while acknowledging that it is a privilege to seek help, and often a lack thereof keeps us from it, too.

I've consoled a client who returned from a hard-won psychiatrist appointment that took great courage to go to after her anxiety almost led to her losing her teaching job. The doctor looked down at her and told her she just needed to exercise and "not worry."

Excuse me, *what*?

I've listened as a client with chronic pain said the doctor told her it was just stress.

I've felt the injustice when a friend of mine, a Black woman, was turned away in an hour of need by a white psychiatrist on a manufactured technicality.

I've talked with a new OB-GYN friend on the phone, telling her how grateful I am to have someone who will listen to the patients I refer to her. "That is so rare," I tell her. As someone who listens for a living, I am aware of how little people who are hurting are listened to.

Has this happened to you? At a doctor's office, a therapist's, at a church, or in a coaching session, or someplace else?

In my opinion, it often happens when mental health, trauma, and emotional suffering are involved. Why? Because these things are layered, often complex in their etiology. Part of the problem is that professionals treating these people want the pain to go away as quickly as possible. Perhaps the patience of these professionals has been worn down over the years, because of the stresses in their own lives or the burden of their own unnamed pain. Maybe their caseload has wearied them, and they just want to leave the office and get home. Whatever the case, they too often cut through the complexity of the problem with a hastily scribbled prescription instead.

When someone says they're sad and can't stop crying, it can be easier to blame them or criticize them than to step back and make space for the potential of trauma history, medical conditions, chemical imbalances, environmental and socioeconomic stressors, and systemic injustices, all of which could be contributing to their pain.

It's a lot simpler to minimize something or spiritualize it, blame the hurting person, or just ignore it all together.

We do that with one another, if we're honest, don't we? How about your friend who has *allllll* the answers? Or that online coach, the one with the teaching videos set to music?

There are "therapists" and "coaches" and "healers" all over the internet, talking about things they don't have the competence, training, or experience to qualify them to address. Too often they oversimplify, and that is appealing to people who are hurting. But when a solution is minimized so that an issue is pared down to an easy 1-2-3 set of steps, it can become harmful.

Most of us have, at some time or another, experienced some version of this. The simplistic solution doesn't work for us, and we are left feeling worse. The truth is that acknowledging the complexity of the problem is where the healing begins. An "easy" solution may sell a lot of books or get a lot of followers on social media, but it can leave people feeling more hopeless and more desperate.

I Don't Know What's Wrong, So It Must Be Me

A wrong diagnosis, label, or understanding is not only harmful, it can also be isolating. At the very least, it can put us on a longer road to finding the right name. At worst, it can cause us to despair about ever finding help.

When we reach out for help and get the opposite, we're left feeling like there's no hope for us.

The terrible consequence of getting a wrong diagnosis, whether from a professional or a friend, is not just that you are not finding the help you need, it's that it often adds to the isolation that comes with the conclusion that it must simply be you, and you begin to feel ashamed.

Shame fuels the narrative that you are suffering, depressed, disappointed, hurt, or anxious because something is wrong *with you*.[1] Shame is never true, but what may be true is that you had valid pains with invalid names.

Identifying that you feel this shame is an important step in finding the correct understanding. This shame isn't yours to carry, and I hope this chapter can take you one step closer to trading in the shame and incorrect diagnoses and labels, for finding more accurate help.

Getting the wrong diagnosis is *dismissal*, not only of our pain but of the reason our pain often goes unnamed. Let's look at that more specifically in the next chapter.

As we do, remember: We are in this together.

CHAPTER 3

IT'S NOT THAT BIG A DEAL— THE HURT OF DISMISSAL

"There's no pain on earth that doesn't crave a benevolent witness."

SUE MONK KIDD

When I was six, I was playing in the cul-de-sac near my house with some neighbor kids. One of them fell down and got pretty badly hurt. He got up and wandered around, crying quietly. The random group of grown-ups and kids didn't seem to know what to do with him. Someone must have called his mom. I saw her walking down the hill. When the boy looked up and saw her, he started wailing as he ran to her, toppling into her arms.

Some might see the child's response as a dramatic attempt to gain his mother's sympathy. That's not what I saw. Deep in my little kid bones, I saw a boy running toward someone who wouldn't dismiss his pain. He was running toward validation and comfort.

That is what we all need when we hurt. Perhaps that is what *you* need.

I can't tell you how many clients I have sat with as they've nonchalantly rattled off an event that happened in their childhood, or as recently as just last week, and I pause them. "Hold on, you're telling me that _____ happened?" I repeat what they shared, making sure I got it right.

They often look surprised, maybe even nervous, fearing I might criticize them for mentioning it or else tell them they're being a little dramatic. They may even say they must be making *too much* of it.

Then I finish my thought... "and it's not *that* big a deal?"

My question may confuse them. They were just reporting information, not expecting to be met with pausing, amplifying, and focusing on what they're saying. Then I say something like, "That is a lot" or "Wow, that sounds really hard" or "That must have been so hurtful" or "I can't believe he said that to you" or simply, "That is not okay."

Sometimes clients will audibly exhale, not realizing they had been holding their breath. Other times, they might say something like, "Yeah, I guess you're right, it is kind of a big deal" or "Yeah, it really did hurt my feelings" or "I thought I was just being dramatic."

Most often, they feel the difference. How did we get there? Neither of us dismissed the experience. We allowed it to be seen, to be heard, to be felt. We allowed it to matter. Why is that important? Because it affects every part of your life.

Regardless of the content, naming their hard experience as *hard* is important. Learning not to dismiss, minimize, or invalidate your experiences is not only essential in naming your pain but in honoring your story.

How We Learned This

Many of us learned to dismiss our experiences from the "teachers" in our lives, as well as from our culture. Both can model this dismissal. Here is what it looks like, sounds like. It's like someone looking away or changing the conversation when your hard thing comes up. It sounds like someone saying to your broken heart, "Well, at least you still have a job." Or if you get a frightening diagnosis, "At least you have health insurance."

Commenting on this, Brené Brown said, "Rarely, if ever, does an empathetic response begin with 'at least'...

Someone just shared something with us that's incredibly painful and...we're trying to put the silver lining around it."[1]

When you hear statements like "at least," you're getting the message loud and clear that you shouldn't focus on the hard thing. This is often someone's attempt to make you feel better, but it has the opposite effect, doesn't it?

Dismissal is more about someone else's discomfort with your hard thing than with the validity of your feelings. Despite best intentions, it leaves you feeling disconnected from that person, isolated, and alone.

I spend a lot of time in therapy not just unpacking hard things but unpacking the way other people have piled more hurt on top of the already hard thing with their dismissal.

The Continuum of Dismissal

I love conceptualizing things on a continuum. Most things are not all-or-nothing. Recognizing that nuance helps us better understand what we are experiencing. It is, in fact, a different kind of naming. In therapy sessions, I often shoot my hands up like goalposts, highlighting the space in between as anywhere you can be with a feeling or an experience.

There are different levels of dismissal, from minimizing to gaslighting. Gaslighting, in case you only vaguely understand it, has an interesting background. It entered our language through a play and its movie adaptation of all things. *Gaslight* was a 1944 film, set in London during the Victorian era. It tells the story of a cunning husband who manipulates his wealthy wife in order to steal her fortune. One way he did this was to alternately dim, then brighten, their indoor gaslights, convincing her she had imagined it and was losing her mind.

It later became a psychological term. Gaslighting is a way to manipulate someone gradually over time by casting doubt on their ability to perceive reality. The result is that the victim unknowingly begins to doubt the accuracy of their own perceptions and the validity of their own thoughts. This can lead to confusion, and greatly impact self-esteem, confidence, and mental health.[2]

These two forms of dismissal—minimizing and gaslighting—exist on a continuum of severity. On the lesser end of the continuum is dismissal, which is sometimes so subtle as to be imperceptible. But even though you can't detect it, it can still be destructive. The severity on this continuum can go all the way to gaslighting someone or even blaming them for their pain. Adding shame to the pain they are experiencing—whether it's a hard day, a hard relationship, or a hard life—only compounds their pain.

Let's now look at the responses your own pain evoked from the people around you. Where do you see your own experiences in these definitions?

Minimizing—When someone tells you it "isn't that big a deal," but it feels important to you.

Example: You share with someone about a hard conversation with your boss, and they say, "You think *that's* bad; you should hear how my cousin's boss berated *her!*"

Dismissing—Your hard thing isn't just minimized, it's brushed off in a condescending, "get-over-it" tone.

Example: You lose your job, and rather than a compassionate response, you are met with "At least you have your health." These "at least" statements are the hallmark of a lack of empathy.

Invalidating—This can occur when you're told that the reasons for the way you feel are not adequate.

Example: You're hurt by a comment at a party and try to confide in a friend, but the response you get is "You're just overreacting. I'm sure they didn't mean it that way."

Spiritual Bypassing—Your pain is bypassed by putting it through a "spiritual lens." In the early 1980s, John Welwood coined the term as a "tendency to use spiritual ideas and practices to sidestep or avoid facing unresolved emotional issues, psychological wounds, and unfinished developmental tasks."[3]

Example: You're trying to have a baby but you are

unable to get pregnant, and instead of empathy, you are met with "Maybe if you stop worrying, it'll happen" or "Maybe God is testing you." You are diagnosed with cancer, and the consolation you get from a spiritual friend is "God has a plan."

Gaslighting—It is in the gaslighter's interest to mislead, confuse, and create self-doubt in whomever they are manipulating. For this reason, it is different in my opinion from the rest of the continuum.

Example: You tell your boss about an inappropriate comment from a coworker, and you're met with "You're just imagining it. There's no way he said that." Gaslighters often know the truth but don't want to be found out or deal with the consequences of the truth being revealed. There is a complicit commitment to this manipulation that makes it different than the rest of the continuum.

A Note About Spiritual Bypassing

This version of dismissing someone's experience warrants further discussion. Spiritual bypassing belongs in the same neighborhood as "everything happens for a reason." It's a place where you are not allowed to feel sad, scared, confused, or uncertain. This misuse of spiritual ideas happens when we avoid facing things in ourselves, or others bypass those things by using spiritual language and popular religious jargon, platitudes, or statements like "God has a plan" and "Just have faith."

It is refusing to recognize hard feelings and unresolved issues by dismissing them with spiritual explanations and sayings. This is not limited to one particular faith or even to faith communities in general. We do this all the time to one another, ignoring the pain by slapping a spiritual label on it.

I once sat across from a couple who was carrying a lot of pain, which, of course, had impacted their marriage. On top of that, the husband had developed such a deep depression that it was affecting his ability to function.

"Accepting this suffering is holy," he told me. "This is the load I have to carry." His wife shook her head, desperate for him to get relief, for both of them to get relief.

I responded as gently as I could. "It isn't holy to keep yourself from help."

It isn't, is it? And yet we do this so often, and in so many ways.

Spiritual bypassing has many forms and faces, but it shares the commonality of making very little of the pain and making a lot of the "shoulds" of how to handle the pain. You know you're being spiritually bypassed when someone glosses over your experience and points to a spiritual or religious solution, or oversimplification, as "one size fits all." There may be great comfort in an anchoring truth, but that never has to include downplaying a hard thing. A spiritual truth, if it is indeed spiritual and indeed true, should be strong enough to anchor the hard things, no bypassing required.

We spiritually bypass ourselves by denying something was hard or rejecting it because it doesn't fit into a neat religious box. When spiritual bypassing comes from other people, or from our community, it can manifest both as the active bypassing of pain and as passive neglect of it. The latter leaves the hurting person alone in a time of great need. Getting to the other side of pain requires people to help us along the way. But when we refuse to engage with things that are messy, we abandon ourselves in our pain.

For example, a young woman sat across from me, mourning not just the marriage she lost but the tight-knit, spiritual community that no longer accepted her. They wouldn't engage with her anymore and looked away as if she wore a scarlet letter on her chest. They took her volunteer position away, leaving her alone in her pain.

I once heard a pastor proudly exclaim about a complicated issue: "We just don't deal with that here."

Well, I thought, *then it sucks to be human here.*

A Different Way

Therapy isn't magic. It has its limitations. But one of the things that good therapy provides is a model for moving toward each other's pain. It's a model of someone seeing you wandering in circles, quietly crying, then walking down the street to embrace you with open arms.

That is such a clear and compelling picture of love, don't you think?

We have a photograph hanging in our house that my husband took of a fire station in London. Written on the building in red letters is: "Love Is the Running Towards."

It isn't more complicated than that.

CHAPTER 4

LISTEN

"The quieter you become, the more you can hear."

RAM DASS

It is astounding the difference a shift from dismissal to validation can make. It's what therapists call a "corrective emotional experience."[1] It helps us learn to relate differently by having the same category of experience in a new way. This can change the way we show up in relationships and helps us feel seen.

But what if you don't have someone who can validate you? What then?

You may not have someone walking down the hill to you today. In fact, that may *be* your pain. But you can walk down that hill to yourself. You can refuse to turn away from your own hurting heart.

Let me be clear. There is no replacement for being with another safe human being.[2] And yet I find we underestimate how we can be with ourselves. I don't think we're taught enough about this capacity for comfort that we all have.

Naming your pain begins with learning to listen to yourself, perhaps in ways you've never been listened to before. You can't name what you can't hear.

I often say to clients, "You are the expert on you." This doesn't mean they understand it all; otherwise they wouldn't be coming to therapy. What it does mean is that you know more about you than I do. You may not know what to call it, but you know more about your life than an outside observer can, especially if you learn to listen.

I believe that God walks down that street toward us, runs even, modeling how we are to love ourselves. Maybe our beliefs on that differ, but regardless, walking down the hill to yourself is the path to learning to listen to what hurts.

A Tiny Revolution

In the early stages of writing this book, a creative bolt of lightning struck me with the best idea. I ran into the house to share it with my husband. Accosting him in the hall, I exclaimed, "I'm going to write an entire chapter." Then I put my hands in the air as if I were writing a Broadway sign. "And I'm going to call it 'Listen.'" I put my hands down, expecting lightning to strike him, too.

It didn't.

He looked at me and blinked. "That sounds great."

"It's about listening *to yourself*," I said passionately.

"That's great."

Great? I thought. *No,* this *changes lives.*

I realize this may seem as unexciting as my husband's response, which is one reason it gets overlooked. Another reason is that it sounds a little cheesy. But stay with me, okay? Because I think it could be a revolutionary shift in your thinking.

We often abandon ourselves at an early age. We do this by minimizing our feelings, either by numbing them or by ignoring them altogether. Feeling something is wrong with us, we learn to present a version of ourselves we think others will accept. And we leave ourselves by choosing to value the opinions of others over our own innate knowledge. Many of us leave early. Some of us are still doing that.

Perhaps one of those who left is you.

Someone once said that the question "what if" is the beginning of every story. I think that is true. Allow me to ask you about *your* story, will you? *What if* you stopped?

What if you stopped leaving yourself? *What if* you went looking for that little girl or boy who was hurt so long ago? *What if* you crested the hill overlooking your old neighborhood and saw the child you once were, wandering around aimlessly, crying? As you open your arms, the child sees you, runs to you, topples into your arms.

How would that change your story?

Listening to yourself is a gentle way of refusing to leave. Just like sitting with a good friend, you don't have to solve everything for them, you simply need to show up.

Leaving my therapist's office in a high-rise office building, I waited for the elevator that led to my own therapy office, several floors below. When I stepped in, I thought about her suggestion for my own pain, *How cheesy*. I pushed the button to my floor. As the doors closed, a second thought came to me. *So helpful, though.* I leaned back against the elevator, reflecting on my therapist's counsel. Before the elevator stopped, I had an epiphany.

I could *be my own friend.*

I could *learn to never leave myself.*

I took a deep breath of that lovely air, held the moment in my lungs, and exhaled. When the elevator reached my floor, I knew, even before the doors opened, that something inside me had shifted.

Now, whenever I find myself facing a hurtful experience, I think, *Here is what I am* not *going to do: I'm not going to* reject myself *when I get rejected. I'm not going to* leave myself *when I feel left. I'm not going to* turn on myself *when I get hurt. I'm not going to* betray myself *when I feel betrayed. I'm not going to* dismiss or gaslight myself.

I've resolved: *I will walk down the hill to me. I will listen. I will be a friend to myself. A good friend.*

I know how grounding it feels to be a good friend to myself. I teach my clients to do the same. I offer you what I have offered them. *You* can be someone who will never leave yourself, who will always be there with an open-armed embrace, who will always be there to listen to the pain of your stories.

You can belong to yourself by validating your own experience. I can't begin to count how many sacred moments of clarity, relief, comfort, grief, anger, and gratitude I have witnessed when someone feels safe enough to stop and listen to what they've been trying to tell themselves. When someone stops writing themselves off, they begin to learn who they are. Which is the direction that you and I are headed. The journey begins with two words: Just listen.

Listen to your body. To your story. To your feelings. To your pain. Listen to the echoes of experiences you were once too afraid to face, or maybe told to dismiss, or that you simply didn't know what to do with. Refuse to look away. Refuse to dismiss yourself in the ways *you* were dismissed.

The relief that listening to yourself brings is life-changing. One of the things I hope you take away from this book is learning to listen, not to me so much but rather *to yourself*.

An important caveat: Some of you may fear that this type of listening could trigger traumatic memories. If so, please reserve this work for a caring professional.

Tell Me More

The best parenting advice I think I have ever heard was: "Tell me more." My son would rattle off something from music class, and I would say, "Tell me more." My daughter would share a playground anecdote, and I would respond with, "Tell me more." It's a simple way to show them I am interested and that I want to learn more. It has served me well, both in my personal relationships and in my professional ones.

At this point, you may be asking: What does it mean to listen to yourself?

It is not unlike "Tell me more." Sometimes, with a hand on my heart, I say something like, "I'm listening." The words may vary, but the intent is the same. Let's look more deeply at the practice of listening by breaking down some of the components.

Curiosity: Maybe you have heard the *Ted Lasso* quote, "Be curious, not judgmental." Why does this strike such a chord with us? In part, I believe it is because we too often lead with judgment, including with ourselves. Nobody likes to be judged. Fear of your own judgment may be one reason you don't listen to yourself. Try being curious instead. Like this: "What am I feeling right now?" Or try putting your hand over your heart and saying, "I'm listening." Curiosity without judgment feels a lot more like love.

Witness: "I see you, I hear you, I believe you. You don't have to prove it to me." That is what it is like to have a validating presence bear witness to whatever experience you have gone through or are going through. This is a gift you can give to yourself. Stop and notice. Stop and notice how you feel when you arrive at work. Stop and notice how your body feels after you get home. Being a witness to your own experiences, regardless of how big or how small they may seem, is a way to honor them.

Validation: Did you know that, even if no one else does, you can validate *yourself*? This doesn't mean you are always right; it merely means you are allowing yourself to honor how you feel. Have you ever found yourself arguing with yourself about whether or not you should feel a certain way? Or arguing a mentally scripted case to prove to someone else that your feelings are valid? A gentle way to sidestep this is to stop arguing and instead acknowledge: *I do feel angry, and it's okay.*

Listening to Your Body: Many of us are more familiar with listening to our feelings than perhaps we are with listening to our bodies.[3] We're often taught to dismiss our body's needs, even the most basic ones, such as needing to eat or go to the bathroom. Listening to your body is also a way of knowing yourself. When clients engage in *being with* their bodies, respecting them with attention, wonderful things have happened. I've seen people learn how to honor their need for rest by tuning in to how exhausted they are. Some learn what they need in a partnership by listening to the needs of their own body. Others have discovered a medical diagnosis by attending to what their body is saying and responding in a way that leads to finding help. It's astounding what you can discover when you listen to your body.

Letting It All Be True: One of the most freeing things is this simple idea I often say in therapy: "Let it all be true." You don't have to choose. It isn't a competition between feelings. We so often feel as if we need to pick one feeling or another, confining us to live in false binaries. "I love this or hate it" or "She's a good friend or a bad friend." The reality is that we may feel fifteen different things at the same time. "I am grateful for my job, and I am bored out of my mind." The relief comes in no longer litigating how we feel but instead allowing it all to exist at the same time.

Listening begets listening. As we pay attention, we become more attentive to ourselves, especially to the parts that are scared, unsure, or needing something from us.

Before we leave this section, I would like to offer a few more hypotheticals for you to consider.

What if listening to and being a good friend to yourself *can* change your life? *What if* it starts a revolution within you to refuse to treat yourself in the hurtful, dismissive ways that you may have been treated?

Research is on the side of walking down the hill and befriending yourself. Bessel van der Kolk, author of *The Body Keeps the Score*, insightfully writes, "Neuroscience research shows that the only way we can change the way we feel is by becoming aware of our inner experience and learning to befriend what is going on inside ourselves."[4]

Your story asks for your attentive friendship. Sticking with yourself is the bridge to naming your pain. Take you *with you* over that bridge. Hold your own hand. And together let's cross over to the place where we can find specific names for your pain.

PART 2

THE JOURNEY– FINDING NAMES FOR YOUR PAIN

CHAPTER 5

SHERLOCKING YOUR LIFE

"The beginning of wisdom is to call
things by their proper name."

Confucius

When I went to see Dr. Barnes in my early twenties, he modeled for me how to pick something up and look at it with new eyes. He and I began to piece together the clues of my story, and, in that process, I began to understand why I was struggling the way I was. The clues were always there. I just didn't have names for them. In their absence, I had accepted shame-based narratives about myself.

In Part 2 of this book, we are going to look more closely at different pains I see in my office. I hope you will discover some of your own clues in this naming process. More than that, though, I hope you will feel better equipped to investigate your own story, whether we name it in this book or not.

A little backstory first. I grew up with a mother who loved mystery shows. I often found myself watching them with her. I find these detective series a helpful metaphor for some of the work I do. Detective shows are compelling because the clues are right there, often under our nose, but annoyingly just out of reach. That is, until Sherlock Holmes (or whichever detective you prefer) enters the story, piecing the clues together in a way that finally makes sense. The quill pen, for example, left on the book on the table in the study was always there, but it meant nothing until its significance was revealed. Once the clue is understood, it leads to another clue, and another, until the entire story makes sense.

Mystery solved.

Let's talk about your own mystery. A series of things *has* happened or *is* happening in your life. The question is why. How has it impacted your life? What do the clues mean? The evidence is there, but without context, like that random quill pen sitting on a book in the study. It may not make sense to you because the narrative isn't clear until the clues are understood.

An unnamed experience from your past can create a

false narrative, telling a story about you that isn't true. It's only by accurately naming the painful experience that you can begin to understand how it has impacted you. When you understand the clues left strewn throughout your life, you can unravel the mystery of why you feel the way you do.

Or as a friend of mine so aptly put it, "To name something is to know it."[1]

When a client comes into my office and unloads a really hard week, dumping all of its contents in the middle of the floor, do we sweep it under the rug? No. Together we sift through it and name what was hard. At the end of the session, the client often says, "I feel so much better, so much lighter."

Did we solve her hard week in fifty minutes? Unfortunately, no. But we succeeded in naming some of the hard parts.

The sorting and naming you are learning to do can not only inform you but also soothe you. In naming what you feel, you are not just solving the clues of your life, you are also learning to regulate your emotions, calming and comforting yourself.[2] It helps to ease the amygdala, which is the emotional part of the brain.

The phrase "name it to tame it," was coined by

psychiatrist Dan Siegel as shorthand for that process.[3] When you name a feeling, the part of your brain naming it sends messages to the part of your brain that feels the big feelings and helps to tame them. So not only does naming help you find what you need, it also helps to comfort you.

Your Brain Seeing Bears

We are going to learn to name things together in this section, but first let's learn a little about how you are wired and what to do if you feel overwhelmed by any feelings that come up—like the following client had to do.

She was a new client, calling in distress to request therapy. Her panic was palpable. She was experiencing anxiety in graduate school in a way she never had before, and it was frightening. Added to her panic, she was afraid she was "losing it." It's scary to feel out of control. It was a lot less scary when she learned that her prefrontal cortex—the part of the brain where logic and reason are housed—was deactivating when she was anxious at school, sending her into a fight-or-flight response.[4] I explained that this new situation, linked with her own unique story, had knocked out her guardrails for handling stress, putting her brain and body into a state of emergency.

As I do with many clients, I had her imagine a bear standing in my office.[5] We both agreed that if one were actually there, we would both panic, fight, run, freeze, or all of the above. I then had her replace that bear with her situation at school. She felt a lot less afraid when she understood what her brain was trying to do: protect her from a perceived threat. Imagine, if you will, a grizzly bear standing at the doorway of the room where you are reading this book. Big, dangerous, and terrifying. Your heart may be beating faster just imagining it. Your brain would bypass all logic and go straight into an emergency response of fight, flight, or freeze. It would not have time for reason. Its entire focus would be getting you to safety.

Sometimes our brains don't know the difference between a bear in the doorway and a topic that feels emotionally threatening. That emotional threat could be a topic in this book, a disagreement with your brother-in-law, or a call from your mom, who has been trying to get sober. When your brain senses danger, it reacts to protect you. The danger doesn't have to make sense. Remember, the logical part of your brain gets deactivated. Whenever this happens, name that it is deactivated and use tools to bring it back online.[6]

Some topics you read in books like this, for example, or memories you reflect on can have your brain seeing bears. That's okay; it's temporary. It will feel less scary if you know what is happening. It is important to respond to those moments by stopping to attend to yourself. The truth is, the part of your brain that is capable of learning from a book, which is the prefrontal cortex, is not active when you see bears. Consequently, you won't get very far by trying to push through your anxiety.

In this state, our brain is dis-integrated, meaning that not all the parts are connected.[7] That's why you can't think clearly when you see a bear, or whatever your equivalent to a bear is. It's not only unproductive trying to push through, it is also not exercising good care for yourself.

Remember the image of walking down the hill to yourself? That's what I suggest doing. Scoop yourself up and give yourself an open-armed embrace. Rest in that embrace until you feel safe.

Stay Within Your Window

So how do you know if your brain is seeing bears? By learning to recognize the signs that you are being knocked out of your window of tolerance.[8] This is a clinical term for an emotional space in which you can feel some stress, but it's not overwhelming. We stay emotionally regulated by staying within our window of tolerance.

Another way to think about the window of tolerance is to picture yourself running on a sidewalk. You have some wiggle room; you can move to the left or right to avoid obstacles in your path. You may trip over a root growing through the concrete, for example, or an upraised seam in the sidewalk. Your situation is not entirely without risks, but it is manageable enough to allow you to keep moving forward with a clear head. Now imagine running off the sidewalk into the busy street. Much less manageable, right? Or imagine running off the other side into the woods. Also less manageable. Both off-sidewalk options present more hazards. Your window of tolerance is what you can feel and manage *while* you're on your sidewalk.

We all have different sidewalks, based on our histories and the coping mechanisms we have developed along the way. Our window of tolerance also varies depending on the topic. For instance, you may have a wide window when it comes to managing stress at work, but quite a narrow window when the stress happens at home. Our windows widen as we learn new coping skills and when the hurting parts of us are healed.

So you have arrived at this point in the book with your current window size. I wouldn't be a very good guide if I didn't equip you to recognize when you are pushed outside your limits and teach you what to do about that. When you find yourself pushed out of your window into a fight-or-flight state, you will realize it because you feel angry, irritable, chaotic, anxious, have racing thoughts, a feeling of hypervigilance, or restlessness. This is an agitated state. Great for reacting to a bear, not for reading a book. On the other side of the window, you may find yourself in a freeze state. You will know you are there when you feel overwhelmed, emotionally numb, lacking motivation, exhausted, even depressed. In short, too stressed to move, either literally or figuratively.

If you find yourself on either side of your window of tolerance, feeling these things, it is a sign to pay attention. It is *not* something to push through. Pause and assess what you need.

Think about it like the indicators on the dashboard of your car. They signal overheating, oil change needed, low on gas. For the car to continue functioning well, you have to honor them.

The same goes for you.

Tools to Reach For

Most public places have a fire extinguisher or a defibrillator behind the plexiglass of a red box, outside of which are the words boldly written: "Break in case of emergency." There are different iterations of this depending on location, all announcing the plan if things get rough. I like to think of mental health tools in the glass container, always waiting there for when you need them. Or maybe what you need is like a device with a GPS, a tool to reach for when you feel lost, pushed out of your window. Or perhaps it's an anchor that you can lower when you feel you are in rough, emotional waters. It's good to have a plan, something to reach for when you are having big feelings.

Here are some of my favorites:

Pause: The simplest thing you can do when you feel triggered or overwhelmed is to stop. I'll give you a hypothetical example. Say you are reading this book and get triggered by something. Simply put the book down. Return to it only with a caring professional or a good friend, when you are feeling more emotionally regulated. Know your limits and honor them.

Grounding: Grounding is a way to bring you back to the present moment by engaging your senses in order to re-integrate your brain. I think of it like connecting to the ground under your feet whenever you feel swept away by some intense feeling.

One technique you may be familiar with is this: Name five things you see, four things you hear, three things you feel, two things you smell, and one thing you taste. Do this slowly and with intention. For some people, finding things you're smelling or tasting can be distracting. If so, I suggest repeating the first three until you feel more present. Name what you see, hear, and feel. Repeat.

You may also just sit with your feet on the ground, your back against the chair, feeling yourself rooted and connected to the earth. Name where you are and that you are safe. When a client needs to get grounded because his feelings are overwhelming, I'll say something like, "Okay, let's take a break. Let's put your feet on the ground. Feel the sofa under you. Take a deep breath. Feel your feet on the ground." The truth is that you can do grounding exercises in any way you like, adapting them to any situation.

Breathing: The secret to breathing in a way that helps you return to your window of toler-ance is to breathe out longer than you breathe in.[9] This longer exhalation is key. This kind of slow breathing, especially on the exhale, sig-nals calm to your body. Try this: Inhale for four counts, hold for four, exhale for six. Another option is the "cyclic sigh" (also referred to as the "physiological sigh"), which research points to as the most calming for your body.[10] Take one inhale, pause, then follow that with another deep inhale through your nose to fill your lungs. Then expel the air slowly through your mouth, pushing it out through pursed lips. Repeat.

Physical Movement: Not everyone is able to use physical movement, but if you can, it takes at least twenty minutes of physical movement to return to a place of calm. This can take many forms, but I find walking the most helpful. This movement tells your brain that you have successfully survived the danger and that your body is now safe.[11]

Self-Hold: I learned about the self-hold in training with somatic therapy expert Peter Levine.[12] He modeled taking your right hand and placing it under your left armpit. You then take your left hand and put it across your chest, like a seat belt, resting your left hand on your right shoulder. Then just hold. Levine teaches that part of trauma is that we lose the boundaries around ourselves. This type of hold helps you feel contained.

Butterfly Hug: The Butterfly Hug is accomplished by crossing your arms over your chest and resting each of your hands on the opposite upper arm or shoulder.[13] Then softly pat your arms or shoulders in an alternating rhythm, calmly patting one side, then the other. You may also overlap your hands, interlocking your thumbs, so that your hands are resting on your chest, and pat back and forth that way, too. This can help you feel grounded and soothed. Keep patting gently, alternating sides, until you feel calmer.

Cool Water: Put your hands under cool, running water. I recommend this to clients for when they are going into anxiety-provoking situations, but it can be used anytime. If you are feeling overwhelmed in a moment, slip into the restroom, turn the cold water on, and for just a few moments let it run over your hands. Pair this also with a grounding statement like "I'm okay" or "I have choices, and I can take care of myself." Drinking ice water can also help bring you back to your body.

Journaling: I know, I roll my eyes at journaling, too. But the thing is, it really helps. It's effective because your right brain has the feelings, while your left brain has the words. Journaling helps integrate your brain by engaging the two sides.[14]

Connecting with a Safe Person: There is no replacement for a safe person. Social engagement is the first instinct for survival when in danger.[15] Call for help.

Why did I include this *last* in your toolbox? Because some of you may not have someone you consider safe yet. But if you do have someone safe to reach out to—and all you need is one—please do so when you are overwhelmed.

Knowing yourself is not simply Sherlocking your story; it is becoming a student of your wiring. From time to time, all of us get knocked off our emotional sidewalk. Fortunately, we can all find our way back on.

Take these tools with you as you journey further into this book. Take them into the office, social situations, and certainly to the next extended family gathering.

CHAPTER 6

REDRAWING YOUR INNER MAP

*"Your task is not to seek for love, but merely
to seek and find all the barriers within
yourself that you have built against it."*

RUMI

I celebrated with a female client as she told me how she had not only found her voice but had also used it in a new way. It was exhilarating for both of us. She had been editing herself out of her voice for so many years that she wondered if she even had one. Recognizing the sound of it now, it felt like freedom.

Where had it been all these years?

She had grown up in a house full of volatile anger. To avoid being a target of her parents' anger, she learned to be as quiet as possible. Any stress her parents had, she was blamed for it. Anytime she expressed her needs, her parents saw it as her problem, not theirs. Understandably, she lost connection to her voice. And then, she did what we all do—she took what had helped her survive her childhood into her adult life. So did the following couple.

I sat across from them in a tender moment of couple's therapy. We had successfully moved through their escalated cycles of conflict and progressed to a deeper level. We were at the place where they were reconnected enough to be able to hear each other's stories in a new way. She struggled to be close to him, hesitant to let him into her thoughts and feelings, while he overwhelmed her with his neediness. This pattern became predictable, cycling into a rut they couldn't get out of.

How did they get here?

We pieced together the clues in their stories. In that environment of tenderness, the wife shared first. She had never had anyone to rely on, she explained, and, in the absence of someone like that, she had to become fiercely independent. It was a strength that served her well in many areas, but it had also become a wall, not only between her and her husband but also between her and everyone else. It was difficult for her to trust him. How could she know he wouldn't leave? With that fear dominating her life, she had concluded that the risk was too great to get close.

As for the husband, he shared that he had had inconsistent attention growing up. The chaos and unpredictability of his home taught him that the "squeaky wheel gets the oil." And so he learned early on that he had to squeak loudly, and often, just to get his mom's attention. Even though his mother had died a long time ago, this pattern became so ingrained in him that he still struggled addressing his needs in an adult manner.

This couple did what we all do. They took what they learned from their families of origin into their adult relationships.

We all originated somewhere, though the specifics may be drastically different for each of us. "Family of origin" is a therapeutic term, pointing to where you came from. Your family is the first social group you encounter; they are the first relationships you engage in. It is *your* origin story. And it leaves an imprint on you that must be explored and understood to comprehend your pain. We all have experiences in our first families, and, unexamined, we draw conclusions from these experiences, not only about ourselves but also about our relationships with others. Those conclusions, whether they are true or false, sketch an inner map that stays with you. Unless, of course, you go back and correct that map.

If your inner map has created pain, then this is your work: to redraw the map that has led you off course. Some of us have maps that led us further off course than others, and everyone's path looks different. But we all have to sift through our early experiences to understand their role in leading us to our current point. Nobody's family is perfect. Some families are pretty great. Others, though, are toxic. Wherever your family falls on this continuum, no one arrives at adulthood unaffected.

Where do I start? you may be wondering. Start with this: You are *not* your family. Their impact on you is linked to understanding who you are today. Keep the good parts of your map in place; redraw the ones that aren't serving you.

You Were Shaped by Necessity

When we are little, we instinctively know that we are dependent on our caregivers for our survival.[1] We realize we have to adapt to whatever our family situation is. This truth alone determines how you will name the pain from your family. Being shaped by necessity allows you to look at yourself today with compassion. Kids know, without being able to express it, that *no one else is coming.* You didn't choose your family. You also didn't choose the pain they knowingly or unknowingly passed on to you. The survival skills you developed in your childhood, although they once served a purpose, likely now serve only to frustrate you.

If you had to adapt to fit in, the pain you name will reflect that. If you had to protect yourself and your siblings from abuse, the pain you name will reflect that, too. There is a continuum of impact that rests on the truth that all of us were shaped in some way to make this first social group as tolerable and safe as possible. Were you accepted when you cried? Encouraged when you failed? Were you blamed for your father's mood?

So, the question isn't *if* you were shaped, the question is *how* and *how much* it has shaped you. The issue isn't if you arrived to adulthood with some pain, the issue is *how much* and *what kind*?

Bessel van der Kolk says it well: "Children have a biological instinct to attach—they have no choice. Whether their parents or caregivers are loving and caring or distant, insensitive, rejecting, or abusive, children will develop a coping style based on their attempts to get at least some of their needs met."[2] The question that will help you name your pain becomes, *Were your needs met?* If they weren't, what did you have to do to try to get them met?

But first, let's deal with a common obstacle to this discussion.

It's Okay to Say It's Not Okay

Oftentimes when naming pain that involves family relationships, it can feel disloyal to name the hard or confusing parts. This is especially true when the narrative around your family is that you had a "good upbringing," even more so if your parents were admired by others. It can feel disloyal to name what you don't like, along with the ways those things have impacted you. For some of you, there's no illusion that things were great, but it may be considered dishonoring to your family to talk about it with others.

It's okay to acknowledge that your family wasn't, or perhaps still isn't, an emotionally safe place for you. It's okay to acknowledge that a relationship, even one that is supposed to be "good," is hurtful. This doesn't make you a bad person. And it doesn't have to make someone your enemy, either. It is just telling the truth.

Why is this so hard for us to say? Because even if the familiar thing is harmful, it's still all that we know. We often install curtains, decorate the walls, and make tea in the places that are familiar to us, even if they feel like a prison. Kids don't have another option; they must make the best of their family. Sometimes we don't outgrow that adaptation. Other times, there is pressure to never admit it.

Acknowledging that someone is responsible for pain in your life doesn't mean you have to do anything drastic. It just means that you are validating what you have experienced. If the experiences in your life mean something different to you than what you were told they mean, it can be liberating for you to validate your own experience. It's okay to tell yourself the truth. It will not only benefit you but also your relationships.

Let me be clear: You don't have to tell *them* the truth. At least, not today. A stereotype about therapy is that if you admit you are mad at your father, you need to write him a letter—and send it. Or call a family meeting and confront him. This is not only inaccurate, it also keeps people from being honest with themselves. This type of overly simplistic thinking assumes that it will be helpful for you to do so. People who hurt you may not be safe enough to discuss the truth with.

I see a lot of exhales when I tell my clients that I am not going to ask them to confront their parents. It takes a lot of emotional health from someone who hurt you to handle a confrontation like this without becoming defensive. This information is just for you. And if you choose to do something with that information at a later time, that will also be up to you.

Why Do Therapists Want to Know All About Your Family?

Why *do* therapists always want to know all about your family?

Because we learn so much about who we are by what is reflected back to us by our first caregivers.

Therapists want to know about your family, not to point fingers, as some fear, but because sifting through your origin story not only helps you understand yourself today but helps lay the groundwork for change.

Regardless of your upbringing, it's possible to change the way you relate to yourself and to others by developing a coherent narrative of your life. A lot of therapy clients have significant pain from their upbringing. Maybe you do, too. But if you're able to make sense of your story by unpacking it, you're more likely to develop a secure attachment with others. And so will your children or future children, if you have them.

Making sense of your story involves what researchers call a "life narrative," shaping how we tell our story to others.[3] According to Dr. Daniel Siegel, those who are able to learn to securely attach "tend to acknowledge both positive and negative aspects of their family experiences, and they were able to show how these experiences related to later development. They could give a coherent account of their past and how they came to be who they are as adults."[4]

When it comes to building secure attachment in relationships, Siegel adds, "having difficult experiences early in life is less important than whether we've found a way to make sense of how these experiences have affected us... [M]aking sense is essential to our well-being and happiness."[5] Naming the good and the pain of your upbringing turns out to be part of the solution. I find the accessibility of that to be incredibly good news. It is in the naming that you pave a new way of being. And who doesn't want that?

Did You Get What You Needed?

After establishing a connection with a new client, at some point I ask them to describe their caregivers. Maybe it is a biological mother, maybe an adoptive or foster parent. Maybe it is a grandmother they spent all their time with while their parents worked.

We go through each person who took care of them, then I ask: "Who did you go to when you were hurting?"[6] This is always the most telling question for me and for my clients. Sometimes the answer is heartfelt, and a client remembers the way her dad listened in the car. Sometimes the lack of comfort is heartbreaking to hear. "Well, no one. I went to my room alone." Or "My mom would get so stressed I couldn't tell her anything."

This discussion quickly leads to other dynamics between you as a child and the caregivers you had. "They never listened," "Everything was about my brother," "We had to be perfect," "I knew about the affair before my mom did."

Here we find the epicenter of family pain: Did you get what you needed? Could they be who you needed them to be?

The truth is, none of us can give our children everything they need. We are all limited. We are all human. Many well-meaning parents can't give their children what they need because of the hardships *they* are experiencing, which have nothing to do with how much they love their children—depression, for example, or a cancer diagnosis, a job loss, or working two jobs to make ends meet. The list that deserves our compassion is endless.

And yet.

Even if your caregivers were doing all they could do, it still may have been hard on you. Remember, it's okay to say what was hard. It's okay to listen to and validate your experience. So *did* you get what you needed? Or, to put it another way, what did you need that they couldn't give you? Finally, what was the story you told yourself about that unmet need?

You are the one who best knows the answer to this question. You know it in your bones, don't you?

So, I ask again, did you get what you needed? Sometimes? Never? Only when you were at Grandma's?

Secure attachment looks like a parent who is able to be warm, sensitive, responsive, and dependable. Not perfect. But tuned in to you and your needs.[7]

In contrast, the pain of an insecure attachment is when you didn't have someone attuned to your needs. Maybe you only had it sometimes, or only with people who weren't family. It's not only painful not to get your attachment needs met, it also shapes how you connect in other relationships.

Remember the idea of your inner map? Think of your specific attachment experience as your inner map. If the map of your childhood isn't carefully studied and the places on it correctly named, it will be more difficult to navigate your adult life. From the earliest, impressionable years, you learned what to expect (or what not to), what you think you deserve (or don't), and what you think is possible (or what isn't).

Carrying these maps around, tucked under your arm, unquestioned, leaves you to repeat them, reenacting patterns you grew up with.

That is, unless you name the map.

Separating Your Lovability from Their Inability

Whatever kind of pain you name from your family, the next step will be learning to separate that pain from your identity. It's essential that we remember to separate your lovability from their ability (or lack of) to love you well. Their inability to love you well is about *them*, not you.

We know that young children are by nature egocentric, meaning that they see only from their point of view, unless told otherwise.[8] Because they don't realize that a caregiver's inability to love them well is not their fault, they often blame themselves.

If we don't separate our lovability from their inability, then we may carry a pain narrative that sounds something like: "If I just_____ ..." or "If I were just more_____ ..." "...then they might love me."

There was nothing you could have done as a child to make them better at loving you. Why? Because the parent–child relationship isn't an equal one. When one person is an adult and another a child, the responsibility for the relationship rests on the adult. So even if you are compassionate, forgiving, and understand why they failed you in the ways they did, the responsibility is on their shoulders, *not yours*. Understanding that interrupts this painful second narrative of wishing you were different so that their relationship with you would be different.

This is a good place to turn away from the love you

didn't get to the love you have to give. Walk down the street to yourself. Open your arms and embrace the little child you once were. Redrawing your inner map is essentially the work of understanding the old one, in order that you can chart a new course.

CHAPTER 7

WHAT DID THEY CALL YOU?

*"Anything or anyone that does not bring
you alive is too small for you."*

DAVID WHYTE

When I was a kid, I had an enormous overbite, a legacy from my thumb-sucking days. My front teeth stuck out significantly until I got braces. I was often made fun of for looking "like a monkey." I can still feel my face getting hot in the computer lab as I overheard a boy hurling this insult my way. The hurtful words of others can linger. For years, even after my teeth were fixed, I would still cover my mouth reflexively when sitting in class.

Fortunately, most kids outgrow their middle-school

cruelties. But not all. Some bullies stay bullies, keeping that part of themselves hidden until needed. Like an agent I met with a few years ago to talk about marketing my work. When I asked for more time to decide about working with him, he told me I was unprofessional. He proceeded to shame me and mock me over email. Why? Because he didn't get what he wanted. I was stunned.

His language was domineering, demeaning, and gaslighting. My husband, sitting next to me, was flabbergasted, furious at the man's language. "Don't dignify him with a response." Now, I *know* the man was wrong, that *he* was the one being unprofessional. And yet still, still! I leaned in for a minute to read the names he was calling me. With each line, my chest grew tighter.

Have you ever found yourself doing this? Your sister-in-law calls you selfish for having a boundary. When you provide feedback for a coworker, she whispers around the office that you're hard to work with. And your friend, you know, the one who never calls, says you're a bad friend when you finally stop making all the effort. You may know you are right, but still you listen, even as you feel your chest getting tighter. Why?

Because these negative words click, even for just a minute, into a false narrative or into a fear you have.

Boundaries were never easy for you to set. It took everything in you to tell your sister-in-law you couldn't make it to a dinner she had planned. She called you selfish for having that boundary. *Is she right?* you wondered. At work you feared being too much, and so giving feedback took all your courage. Is it true what your coworker said behind your back? Are you hard to work with? Should you keep your ideas to yourself? You've always wanted to be a good friend, tending to pick friendships where *you* do most of the work, a legacy from your people-pleasing childhood. You finally stopped over-functioning in this relationship, so this is a significant divergence from your norm. Does that make you a bad friend now?

The click for name-calling depends on a preexisting fear you are carrying. Though an inaccurate one, it is a painful one.

The Hook

This agent's insults had found the smallest opening in an old narrative of mine. I feared I wasn't good enough for the work I was hoping to do, and that he, with his connections, would get me kicked off the metaphorical therapist/writer island. What got my attention was not the credibility of his claim, it was my lack of confidence. I didn't listen because I thought he was right. I listened because I subconsciously feared getting kicked off the island. *Maybe I am* not *good enough to be there.* For a moment, I feared that this angry man with narcissistic traits somehow had the power to vote me off. I got hooked, not by the validity of his words but by the vulnerability of my triggers.

Sometimes the hook is what gets you, not the name. When you find yourself listening to an insult in spite of your better judgment, you may be caught by a hook.

A hook is "a selling point or marketing scheme."[1] People often define it as the part of a book that grabs your attention. A hook is also something that is used to catch things. It is meant to ensnare. The names you are called sometimes have hooks in them. They sink into a fear that you are carrying. The more specific the hook is to your fear, the more attentively you will listen to it. And the more flesh a hook can sink into, the more likely it is that you will be caught.

The ways we try to unhook ourselves are often ineffective. "Who cares what anyone thinks?" is a popular mantra today. That's often the model used to stand up to these insults. This is unrealistic. We try to say, "Who cares," but most of us know in our bones it doesn't work.[2] And the reason we can't just shake it off is not because we care too much what other people think. It is because the hook got us. It attaches to whatever hurtful narrative is currently active or unresolved. The pain of name-calling in these scenarios is not about the name, it is about the fear it activates.

Part of what helped me unhook myself was identifying how my old pain narratives were activated and verbalizing what I was feeling. I was creating a whole story about the worst thing that could happen, a far-fetched fear that this rude man would get me kicked off the island. It wasn't even about the things he called me. Saying this out loud helped me hear how ludicrous my fear was. I emailed him back a more accurate summary of *his* behavior, and I unhooked myself.

It is not eliminating the hook that helps us wriggle out of this pain; it is naming the spots it catches. It's identifying out loud the false belief the hook has snagged. As you acknowledge the hurtful things you have been called, explore whether any of them have a hook. Uncovering the pain is not just remembering the insult, it is bringing the place it hooked into the light.

What are the names and hooks that *you* remember?

The Stickiness of Shock

When my daughter was in first grade, another little girl pointed at her legs and said, "Big." It was clear from her tone this was not a good thing. This was a new idea to my daughter, and for a while "big" stuck. Thankfully, it didn't grow into a dislike of her body. But it did present a new question: *Is this true?* In that moment, an innocence about her legs was lost. Name-calling can stick because a part of our innocence gets destroyed. In our house, her main incubator up until that point, there was never a discussion about the size of body parts. The novelty of that girl's comment caught her attention, and the shock of this is what made it stick.

A critical comment can stick when it blindsides us, altering how we see ourselves. When this happens and we don't have a box for it, we wonder, perhaps for the first time, *Do they know something* I *don't know? Have I been naïve this whole time to a reality everyone else believes about me?*

This happens all the time online. Someone who doesn't know you lobs a remark at you, and the shock of it, like cold water on your face, causes you to pause and consider it. On an Instagram live discussion with another writer, a stranger popped into the chat and said, "Monica is full of s—." The comment just sat there, literally written across my online face. Now, I may have been called names before, but being told I was "full of s—" was not one of them. I was mortified. My face flushed, and my stomach dropped. The novelty of it was partly why it was sticky. It was so unexpected that, ironically, I listened.

Identifying the shock, what it changed about your worldview and self-view, even temporarily, is part of unhooking yourself, too. As we sit with the ugliness of what we've been called, it is helpful to understand that we may be mistaking the novelty of the assault for knowledge. But novelty is not knowledge. And the pain lobbed at you actually has everything to do with the caller and nothing to do with you.

Hate and Name-Calling

In middle school a boy called me a "half-breed" racial slur to my face that targeted my Spanish-American heritage. I was standing next to another student, a boy with skin darker than mine, and after the classmate spat this insult at me, he spat something similar at him. It embarrassed me in front of my class. However, with my white skin and the privileges it afforded me, I knew, without being able to articulate it, that this racial slur was more dangerous for the boy next to me. I instinctively knew this name-calling could be signaling more hatred and harm to come for him. He would likely face discrimination; I would not. He could be in danger; I would not be. These are not the same thing. I share this story to highlight that distinction. I didn't have the words then for how being white shielded me from so much hatred in society. But I do now.

Not all name-calling is the same. Name-calling can be truly dangerous, and it is important to highlight that. Name-calling can represent violence or incite violence.

It can carry the hatred and injustices that so many face every day. Words try to cut away at your right to belong, at your right to be treated equally, and your right to be treated with respect. Those words threaten your safety in a moment, in a group, in a classroom, in an office, or your place in society. Name-calling is also often used to deny the dignity you deserve and to label you as "other" or ostracize you. The intent is to belittle, to abuse, to oppress, to separate, or to inflict pain. Words filled with hatred, racism, homophobia, transphobia, ableism, misogyny, and more carry weight that is historical, going back generations. They are freighted with years of injustice and violence. Calling anyone a hateful name, whether online or in person, is dangerous. There is also danger that comes in *not* combating this. As you examine your own experiences with this form of bullying, the larger societal culprits must also be called out.

What Did They Call *You*?

Revisiting these places is painful. Name-calling cuts into the fabric of your sense of self. It attempts to tear your worth. It can hook into a fear or shock you into listening. It can also be full of hate. As you reflect on the names you have been called, I want to leave you with an image, one that I hope will be encouraging and comforting as you do this hard work.

You are walking down the hill to yourself again, only this time you are surrounded, not by neighbors ineffective at comforting you but by the people who have called you terrible things. You wipe your hands on your apron, pull back your hair, and head toward the crowd. Your walk becomes a jog, then a run. You break into the group and find your hurting self in the middle, spinning around, listening to the jeers. Not wasting any time, you pick yourself up, throw yourself over your shoulder, and push your way out of the circle, too busy breaking out to even look back. You whisper confidently as you push out, "This *never* had anything to do with you. It was about *them*."

You arrive at the top of the hill, exhausted but relieved. Your hurting self looks back. The group, filled with the noise of your hurts, is turned in on itself, still going! You are outside of it now, marveling at how they haven't even noticed that you are no longer there. Then it hits you. The abusive names were never about *you*. They didn't even originate with you. The hurtful words hurled and still going will be there whether you are there or not, because the name-calling is always about the heart of the one saying the hurtful things, not the recipient.

CHAPTER 8

IS THIS TRAUMA?

*"If we want to understand the oak, it's
back to the acorn we must go."*

OPRAH WINFREY

How do you feel when you read the word *trauma*? Do you nod in recognition of the trauma in your story? Or do you feel unsure about what qualifies it? Do you reject it, certain that your pain doesn't qualify as "real" trauma?

Trauma is more common than we realize.[1] Even though it has become a buzzword these days, it remains somewhat a mystery because our understanding of it is limited. Trauma is an overused word, but that doesn't always translate into an effective understanding. In fact, we use the word so often now that, in many cases, it has lost its meaning. As a result, we can lose our understanding of ourselves, too. Whether your story carries trauma or not, understanding this pain will help you understand yourself and the world around you more.

So let's take a step back before we hold up parts of our stories and ask the question, *Is this trauma?*

Let's revisit the idea of Sherlocking your life. Remember the clues? The quill pen, lying on the book that is sitting on the table in the study. Because they may mean more than they appear, all clues are to be explored. Look around the room. There is something you didn't notice before—a tangled ball of yarn on the chair next to the table. *Why is it tangled?* you ask.

You have to unwind it to understand it.

Start there.

Even though the clues may seem to have nothing to do with one another, or like a confusing knotted jumble, they might be connected. Say the clues in your life are sleeplessness, depression, chronic pain, and fatigue. Or perhaps addictive behaviors. Maybe even panic attacks, shame. Seemingly unconnected, right?

You may experience a daily hypervigilance, always feeling on edge, finding it hard to relax. There may be a lack of meaningful boundaries. Possibly low-grade anxiety. Certainly, these symptoms could stem from other sources, but trauma can be overlooked in our investigation. Collectively or individually, these symptoms may be the remnants of unresolved trauma.[2]

These symptoms remain because the messages your body was giving about trauma were not attended to. Why? Because you didn't know what was happening, what you needed, or you didn't have access to help. To survive traumatic experiences, you were likely disconnected from yourself. Your experiences may have isolated you from others as well. Trauma expert and author Peter Levine summarizes it well: "When our bodies are feeling uneasy, they give us messages. The purpose of these messages is to inform us that something inside doesn't feel right, and needs our attention. If these messages go unanswered, over time, they evolve into symptoms of trauma."[3]

You can't answer your body's message with the right response until you know what it is telling you. So it is with unnamed trauma. We respond to the messages that have become symptoms by going back to the beginning. Symptoms that are not resolving may have a source that you haven't yet considered.

The greatest mystery many will uncover in their story is that what they experienced was, in fact, trauma. This is not an unassisted scavenger hunt, though. I am not suggesting looking for things you are unaware of. What

I *am* suggesting is that you often do not know that what you have experienced may be classified as trauma, leaving the clues unsolved and yourself ineffectively cared for. You must have the right name to find the right care.

So What Is Trauma Exactly?

In my work with clients who are healing from trauma, we may start with identifying their lack of awareness that what they have experienced in their life qualifies as trauma. Consequently, some of the struggles they are experiencing are connected to that trauma. Let's start our investigation by asking: *What is trauma?*

Trauma is the wide spectrum of experiences that trigger a variety of responses in the body. Stress and trauma exist on a continuum. Trauma is a ramped-up version of stress in the body when a perceived threat is experienced. How each of us responds to a stressor will be unique, informed by our life experiences, the narratives overlaying them, and our genetics.[4] Therapist and researcher Dr. Hillary McBride explains, "A stressful event becomes a trauma when we feel overwhelmed and powerless. *Trauma* is a Greek word that means 'wound.' In the therapy community, trauma is defined by how a person experiences an event, not by the event itself."[5]

Trauma is not the traumatic event, *it is your body's response to it.* Therefore, one person might experience trauma from something another person didn't. It's wasted time to litigate the size, type, or validity of an event as trauma or not, *when the answer to whether or not it was trauma is embedded in your body's response to it.*

There are many definitions of trauma, but a general consensus is that trauma is something that overwhelms your ability to cope with the experience in the moment. It's something that takes away your empowerment. I often think of it as something that's too big, too hard, or too confusing for the circuitry you are wired with. Sometimes it is a chronic experience. Other times, it is one event.

When my son got a severe concussion, the doctor compared the physical trauma to lightning hitting a house. It was too much, and his body had to react to the impact. With too much electricity running through the circuits, the wiring has to adapt fast to survive by going into a fight/flight/freeze response, or else the house will go up in flames. If not properly addressed, these responses can continue long after the lightning strike.

With my son's concussion, we were instructed to keep him in a darkened room with no stimulation for days until his symptoms disappeared. We had the luxury of not only knowing what had happened but also knowing what kind of care to give him. But what if we hadn't? Those messages of traumatic impact on his brain would have given way to more symptoms later. They could have turned into long-term concussion symptoms like dizziness, anxiety, headaches, and difficulty in concentrating.

Without this knowledge, it may have become a Whac-A-Mole situation where we chased down each symptom, not realizing that the story could be traced all the way back to the concussion. This physical trauma shows what can happen with unnamed trauma in our lives. We try to solve a random persistent symptom, or many symptoms, while missing the origin story of it all. Most of us do not have a clear-cut story like my son's concussion. Instead, we feel more like that tangled ball of yarn.

If that is how you feel, what do you do?

You patiently unwind your story and learn more about how to name your experiences.

You may be familiar with the language of "big T" trauma and "little t" trauma. Big T trauma usually refers to those things you already associate with trauma: violations of a person's body; war; natural disaster; severe emotional, physical, or sexual abuse; violence of any kind; life-threatening illnesses or accidents. Little t trauma is used to refer to things that don't involve violence or disaster, but nonetheless have a significant impact. For example, things like growing up in a high-conflict family, emotional neglect, frequent criticism or humiliation, the loss of a parent, being bullied, medical procedures, minor car accidents, or food insecurity.[6] It's not that these are small experiences; it's that their impact is underestimated. I like to think of trauma as a continuum between the two t's. Your experiences with, say, racism, neglect, or verbal abuse may fall somewhere on the continuum.

Here's the most important thing to remember: Traumas across the continuum can have the same impact on a person. Any type of trauma affects the way our bodies and brains respond, no matter what their perceived severity is. The accumulation of what people refer to as little t traumas over time can be as significant as a big T trauma. Therapist and author Aundi Kolber insightfully describes big T trauma like a deep knife wound: It obviously sends you to the emergency room. However, cumulative little t traumas may be more like paper cuts. One is not such a big deal. But thousands of paper cuts left untreated? That can lead to infection, landing you in the emergency room just like that knife wound did.[7]

As you reflect on these expanded definitions of trauma, what clues in your present-day life are you more curious about? Are there knots in the yarn that may be tied to trauma? How can you unwind your story and gain a better understanding of yourself?

Trauma and the Brain

What happens if our story has been impacted by trauma? It can change the brain's wiring, which is another reason it is essential to identify trauma accurately.

Researcher and clinician Dr. Bruce Perry describes how no one returns to exactly the same shape after a trauma. This doesn't mean that there isn't the possibility of healing and resilience. It does mean, though, that it will come in a new shape. He describes the old idea of resilience that we once held like a soft Nerf football. You squeeze it, and it pops back to its previous shape. This is an inaccurate understanding of resilience after trauma. Instead, he compares it to a wire hanger. If you undo the shape of the hanger, you can return it to its hanger shape, but it will never be exactly the same.[8]

You don't just "go back to normal" after a trauma. You have to find a new normal in order to heal. When people understand this, they are less likely to expect an unrealistic "bounce-back." They begin to attune their expectations more accurately, placing less pressure on the healing process and learning to care for themselves in a more effective way.

What can you expect in addressing your own experience of trauma?

Although the old neural pathways in your brain were made by past traumas, new neural pathways can be created beside them. Regarding the practice of trauma therapy, Dr. Perry writes: "Therapy is more about building new associations, making new, healthier default pathways. It is almost as if therapy is taking your two-lane dirt road and building a four-lane freeway alongside it. The old road stays, but you don't use it much anymore."[9]

The new roads you build—new associations, new ways to feel and maintain safety, increased boundaries, reconnecting with yourself—answer the messages your body was sending for help with invitations to healing.

Unwinding Your Story

Let's go back to the study and look again at the ball of yarn: The loose end is knotted. There are knots throughout. It may look overwhelming to unwind. But yarn cannot tangle itself without someone pulling it. If yarn is not carefully guided out of a ball, it may easily tangle. Our lives and development also require attentive care, but sometimes traumas (a single incident or a chronic series) interrupt this. Many lives are not cared for with such intentionality, encountering instead caregivers who are too unwell to do so. Many lives are treated like yarn yanked from its source. Traumas cause great pain, resulting in what looks like a tangled series of knots. Unnamed traumas can leave us feeling like we have been knotted up in ways we never wanted or chose.

What if the yarn could be unwound, inch by inch? Its unraveling would reveal the story of how the knots were formed. It would reveal why the yarn keeps getting caught. Unwinding it to the beginning reveals what has happened. As a result, it gives the yarn another chance to be rewound in a way that creates fewer knots. When you unwind your past story, you discover the meaning of the clues you see today. You name them properly—and you begin to understand what you need to do to smooth out the knots.

Naming the pain of trauma is not an ending, it's *an invitation*. You can't undo what you went through, but you *can* understand it and attend to it. You may see yourself in the wound-up ball of yarn, full of tangles and knots that don't make sense to you, frustrating you and causing you additional suffering. You may have blamed yourself for the knotted situation you find yourself in. What works better is to pick up the ball of yarn with love, compassion, and curiosity. This is a way of reconnecting with yourself. At the heart of trauma is disconnection created within ourselves and with others. This step, though small, will begin to change your story.

Unwinding your story is a process. Where did the tangles appear? And when? What caused the knots? Are there experiences that never got properly named? Could it be that the tangles make more sense than you once realized? The answers to these questions will lead to the answer of a bigger question: *Is this trauma?*

If your awareness has increased in this chapter and you've discovered that you have significant trauma in your story, the invitation should include the care of a professional therapist. Therapy won't undo past trauma, but it can help build new roads for you to travel. Along the way you can find a new understanding for your life, along with a renewed hope for the journey ahead. (For further exploration, there are curated resources in the library online at monicadicristina.com.)

Notes about trauma: It is often said that you never know the battles someone else is fighting. To this truth I would like to add a few thoughts of my own.

You also never know how quietly courageous someone is being. Sometimes the bravest things you're doing go unseen.

It is brave for you to unwind your story.

It is brave to learn what to name it and what you need.

It will take courage to unwind, untangle, and rewind your story.

It may also take an ally to help.

The messages that may have turned into symptoms may also be invitations to healing for you.

CHAPTER 9

THE LONELINESS IN GRIEF

"I sat with my anger long enough until she told me her real name was grief."

C. S. LEWIS

In his book *A Grief Observed*, C. S. Lewis describes the loss of his wife: "Her absence is like the sky, spread over everything."[1]

For many who are experiencing grief, it is just that, like the sky, covering everything. And yet days continue. On the way to my office, the sun comes up again. It's another day and another session with grief. I walk into the hall to meet my clients. Their loss is fresh, raw, unbearable. They are without words. I greet them quietly. They nod, attempting a smile, as I usher them into my office.

I sit with them in their grief, in their tears. Nothing more can be done at the time.

Henri Nouwen wrote this about such a time: "Learning to weep, learning to keep vigil, learning to wait for the dawn. Perhaps this is what it means to be human."[2]

Dawn comes. The sun comes up another day, another session. We sit together. Again. And again. I wouldn't tell you what it's like to love someone, and so I won't tell you what it's like to lose someone. I have a deference to grief and to those who carry it. I can't describe what it feels like to lose someone irreplaceable, but I have sat with clients grieving spouses, siblings, babies, children. I have sat with those grieving losses they weren't sure they would survive, *could* survive. I can tell you this, though: Their pain is palpable.

Do I lead them out of it?

No. I have learned to honor their grief by following *their* lead.

Grief is a pain we can't solve. Instead, we honor it by naming it and attending to it. I will not attempt to describe what you feel in the aftermath of the devastating loss of a loved one who can never be replaced. How can I describe the whole sky to you, gray and low and stretching from one horizon in your life to another?

Your grief has no clues to overturn. Its presence is undeniable. It announces itself from every empty corner. There is no need for interpretation.

The cousins of this grief, though, are different and subtle, and it is those we often miss but call for our investigation. They're on the table, but they're being called something else.

Grief is not limited to the traditional and sometimes oversimplified ways we define it. I often find myself saying to a client describing a complex pain, "I believe what you're describing is grief." Sometimes they're surprised; usually they're relieved.

Too often, we leave one another alone on the bench of grief. The space on the bench marks the loss, and also the place we should be filling in support. I hope this chapter will help name griefs that may surprise you, shedding light on the loneliness that often accompanies it. In that process, I hope you will feel less alone.

Let's start there.

The Loneliness

From where I sit as a therapist, I see a lot of lonely people. But my anecdotal experience isn't isolated. It's validated by the research. The year I am writing this book the Surgeon General of the United States came out with an alarming report: Loneliness is a public health crisis of epidemic proportions.[3]

I listen as a young couple grieves, no longer able to talk to their parents without the conversation turning to conspiracy theories. "We used to be close," they say, and I can hear the sadness in the words. Many have lost friends, communities, and relationships because of the polarization that occurred in their communities in recent years. A woman describes how her family doesn't know what to do with her divorce. "It's like they can't handle it," and there is loneliness in her voice as she says this.

People are lonely because they are going through something that no one around them can relate to—a divorce, the loss of a child, a serious illness. They are lonely because they have moved to a new city, perhaps, or have left a close-knit group. Suddenly, no one is around. A young woman grieves the church community she lost along the way as her beliefs evolved. "I couldn't stay anymore," she mourns, "but I still miss them, some of them, anyway. It hurts that no one reached out to ask why I left."

Loneliness can feel like a dull ache. But it can have an edge, too, that pierces you sharply, like when you reach out to someone, someone you thought was a friend, and you don't hear back from them.

Loneliness itself is a grief. And when the lonely grieve their loneliness, it can feel like you carry a truth about the world that people are afraid to talk about, fearful of even being around.

Perhaps I am describing the unnamed grief that you are carrying around, which seems too deep for words. I don't want you to be alone in this. Together, we can find those words and name that grief.

Allergic to Grief

When you are allergic to something, you try to avoid it. You do what you have to in order to protect yourself from getting too close to the triggering agent.

We live in a society that is allergic to grief.

Lewis wrote his observations about grief under a pseudonym. It wasn't until after his death that his name was attributed to the book. Although no one knows for sure, some have wondered if he did so because he feared it would be too much for his faithful readers. Regardless of the answer, the question points to our relationship with grief and how we try to soften it. We live in a world that treats unfiltered grief as too much. Too much of a challenge to ideas about God. Too many unresolved questions. Too raw an exploration of pain. Too honest.

Lewis knew what many of you know, too: We don't do grief well.

The sun came up. Another day, another session. A client came to my office for his regular appointment. We sat on the bench of grief again, together. It had been a couple years since he had lost his wife, and we talked about the upcoming reminders of her absence. This was his second season facing them. There were so many this time of year. The day he lost her, her birthday, their son's birthday. It all felt too much. "I just wish people remembered." Occasionally someone would ask about her, how *he* was doing, or his son. But mostly, his entire community seemed to move on, leaving him sitting on that bench, alone.

When someone loses a baby, a spouse, a child, a parent, a sibling, the loss is undeniable. At first, people draw close. But then, a few weeks go by, a few months, a year, even two. When someone gets divorced, falls ill, or is caring for a sick family member, people, however supportive, move on.

Are they trying their best? I believe so, most of the time, anyway. But that doesn't change the impact. Their leaving only accentuates the loss. It can start to feel as if they are allergic to your grief. They just don't want to be around it or bring it up. Clients report being told a version of the same thing: "I was afraid to bring it up, because I didn't want to remind you of it." A grieving person, though, doesn't have the luxury of forgetting their loss. This can start to feel like pressure to "be okay again." It can feel like you're not "moving on" fast enough. The grief is hard enough, but the sense that you are somehow not getting it right only adds to an already heavy burden. It can feel like everyone has scattered when you're still on the bench. The loneliness amplifies the pain.

Grief in Waiting for an Unknown Outcome

It is not just that others are allergic to our grief; oftentimes, we fail to recognize the ways we are indeed grieving. In difficult experiences, there are clues that have to be turned over, examined, and given their valid name—grief.

The grief of waiting for an unknown outcome often accompanies an infertility journey or a medical diagnosis. "If you knew how this story ended," I often tell my clients, "this would feel different. It's the *not knowing* that amplifies the grief."

"This is so hard," one client admitted, sighing as she plopped down on the sofa. She was back in the waiting again, wondering if this time would be different. She wondered if she would be able to get pregnant.

When you don't know how the story will end, the waiting can be an *active grief*. It lives and breathes, accompanying you everywhere—to work, to a baby shower, a family gathering. All the while it casts shadows over your days. You may still cling to some hope, but on many days the sadness overshadows it.

This unwanted companion can shadow your interactions, too. It's exhausting to give the updates—and too vulnerable. You're weary of the questions. You're happy for your friends who have had their happy endings, but your life feels so different from theirs, so much lonelier, sadder.

What you are feeling is grief. And it's okay to feel it. In fact, it's *essential* to feel it.

Grief in Unmet Longing

As your story continues, an unknown outcome turns into an unmet longing. The longing to be in a romantic relationship, for example, or to have a child or a family becomes the backdrop of your life. There are so many wonderful desires that, for no explainable reason, go unfulfilled. You are on the bench, hoping to be seated somewhere else, with your longing fulfilled. But it goes unmet.

I name this with a hurting client. "If I could, I would make this happen for you. I would push that button right now. I don't understand it, either." I acknowledge there is no brilliant therapeutic advice that can solve this unmet longing. The thing she longs for isn't happening, and it hasn't been for years.

We sit on that bench together.

She has prepared that seat for a special someone who hasn't shown up, may never show up. We refuse to put a silver lining on it. The way we dignify her grief is by refusing to use platitudes to soften the reality of her pain. It sucks. It's hard. I assured her that it's okay to feel sorrow, okay to feel angry.

After some digging, you will often discover that under the anger lies a great grief.

Grief in Living Relationships

What is surprising to many people is the connection between grief and anger. I encourage clients to listen to their anger. I find if you listen to your anger, it will usually lead somewhere, sometimes somewhere unexpected. Anger is considered by many a secondary emotion, meaning there is always something underneath it.[4] It often surprises clients how much anger they have toward the people who raised them. But what is even more surprising is the grief under the anger. They grieve the love they never received, grieve the people their parents never were, maybe still aren't. The mom who can't stop talking about herself long enough to take any interest in you, *her child*. The dad who can't stop working, or drinking, or watching TV in order to be there for you, *his child*.

If grief is a bench, sometimes in your anger you kick it over. Once you recognize the sadness under that anger you may pick up the bench you kicked over, sit down, and honor that this, too, is grief.

I remember the tears of a friend, lamenting who her

family wasn't and still isn't. "Why don't they care more? Why don't they ever call? I really just don't get it." She has a family, but do they have her?

Grief in relationships can apply to people who are still living but are no longer a part of your life. Friendships, for example, can implode, or sometimes they just fizzle. There's a hole left where there was once a significant attachment. You may scroll through their social media posts or cross paths at the grocery store. The pain you feel is not just emotional; sometimes it is physical. That's because our brains register disconnection and rejection in the same way as physical pain.[5]

Sometimes we grieve over disappointments, such as discovering someone is not who we thought they were, or over broken trust when a marriage ends because of infidelity, or a friendship ends because of jealousy.

You may grieve someone who is still in your world but has dramatically changed, possibly in ways that they couldn't control. From addiction to a traumatic brain injury, or dementia, this person is no longer the same, and you feel powerless to get as close as you used to be to them. You grieve the loss of who this person once was in your life.

You Can't "Fix" Grief

Grieving can be like sitting on a bench in the middle of a bustling city. Buses pass, horns honk, people hurry by. But the rush of the city seems far away when you're on the bench, because on the bench of grief, time stands still.

The sun comes up again. Another day. Whatever type of grief it is—loneliness itself, unknown outcomes, unmet longings, grieving those still alive—you still sit there. Too often, you are sitting alone. Stepping out of the rush of life to sit with someone in the standstill of grief is connection.

Sitting beside them on that bench is love.

When you refuse to leave them sitting by themselves, when you sit with them, keep vigil with them, and reach out your hand to hold theirs, you're telling them, "You are not alone here."

If, as you read this, you are alone in your grief, I hope you have felt that someone is sitting on that bench with you today, if even for just a moment.

CHAPTER 10

UNDERNEATH THE ANXIETY

*"It is not the thing you fear that you must deal
with, it is the mother of the thing you fear."*

David Whyte

While grief is a pain we *must* weather instead of relieve, anxiety is a pain we *mistakenly* weather instead of relieve.

My husband and I were getting away for the first time as parents of three young children. Instead of celebrating, though, I found myself picturing the plane going down and us dying, leaving our children without their mom and dad. A terribly unromantic thought for such a romantic trip, right? It was stealing my excitement. Like many of you, I was functioning just fine, but I would rehearse this tragedy in my mind as the day approached.

When I shared this with my therapist, she pointed out that I was moving into anxiety to get away from my feelings of vulnerability this trip raised. *Rude*, I thought jokingly. I felt exposed, at first, until I realized she was right. It did feel incredibly vulnerable leaving my children, and it also felt vulnerable doing something so fun. Rather than feel those vulnerable things, though, I resorted to a familiar way of coping: anxiety.

This unlikely example points to what we will uncover beneath your anxiety. For there is always something hiding there, just under the surface. But first, let's make some distinctions. *Everyday anxiety* differs from an *anxiety disorder*. Although this chapter can be applied to any level of anxiety, I recommend seeing a professional if you are experiencing anxiety that is intense, interferes with your regular activities, and lasts for several months or more. This level of anxiety is not situational and may be part of an anxiety disorder that is best served with professional help.[1] Anxiety, a diagnosable disorder or not, can be created by any combination of genetics, trauma, hardship, stage of life, relationships, family of origin—you name it.

We too often see anxiety as the problem when it may be the symptom of a deeper one. For instance, unresolved trauma can cause anxiety.[2] It did in my case.

Anxiety gets mistaken as the main problem, because it's often the loudest one. But it's often an expression of something else underneath that also needs attention. Anxiety is referred to by some theorists as a way of coping.[3] In other words, we use anxiety to cope with something else. Even though it might feel bad, anxiety may be serving a purpose to help us get through something, to avoid something, or to escape feeling something.

Jumping Up Out of Vulnerable Feelings

Just like my example above, many of us pop up and out of our feelings into anxious thinking.

Picture your feelings like a river and your anxious thoughts like birds circling above. If you chase the birds in the sky, you may miss the answers that are floating in the river. Even though anxiety can be exhausting, we find ourselves up there chasing birds because we don't want to, or know how to, feel what's in the river.

This is an automatic response that you are not aware of. For example, you may be feeling sadness you don't want to feel, or even feeling unexpectedly happy. Uncomfortable with these feelings, you pop up and out of the feelings into anxiously chasing birds. When you find yourself stuck in anxious thoughts, it may be helpful to get curious and try to name what you're feeling underneath your anxiety.

Regarding the vulnerability of feeling good things, Brené Brown coined the term "foreboding joy."[4] This is the phenomenon of feeling something blissful and immediately picturing terrifying things happening. Brown describes this with examples like standing peacefully over your baby's crib, only to picture something awful happening. Or the perfect holiday car ride, with holiday songs playing: 60 percent of us will, according to her research, picture a car crash as the next scene, while another 10 to 15 percent picture something equally awful. Citing the intolerance of vulnerability as the core of many anxieties, she says that the joy is just too vulnerable for us to stay in.

Brown recommends *feeling* the vulnerability of the joy of the moment, engaging in gratitude for the joy as a way to stay present. That will keep your mind from imagining worst-case scenarios. Her recommendation to stay with vulnerability works with any feeling you are trying to escape. So whether it is a good feeling or a hard feeling, naming it, and staying with it, can help.

The Lurking Secondary Fear

Anxiety can be fueled by a combination of fearing the worst and underestimating your ability to handle that worst-case scenario. This tendency to overestimate what you fear and underestimate yourself is often at the root of anxiety.[5] You're anxious about something, and you're afraid you won't be able to handle it.

Some version of this is underneath many of our stuck places with anxiety. I want to be clear that I am not minimizing the tremendous weight, fear, and losses that anxieties parade in front of us. But if you experience things that are heartbreaking, these thoughts will not make them easier. In naming this lurking secondary fear, you are less likely to spend your days rehearsing these fears.

Underneath so many of our fears in life is the fear that we will be destroyed, broken beyond repair. It's an existential fear that lurks underneath our anxieties. Yes, the thing you obsess over is worrisome, but the reason you're anxious about it before it happens is likely because you fear you can't handle it. Shoring up the truth, the support, the faith, and the plans for you to effectively deal with it can relieve you of those anxious thoughts.

More immediate than this existential fear is the daily one that you can't handle what is coming your way *today*. Like the fear a client of mine had: Her career was skyrocketing, which created more opportunities and more exposure to larger audiences, often with higher-ups in the company. With this meteoric rise came a crippling fear. She feared feeling anxious in a presentation and *not being able to handle it*. You can imagine the dread this created before presentations. It quickly became paralyzing.

What helped was focusing on the lurking secondary fear: that if she felt anxiety, she wouldn't be able to handle it. We practiced the grounding truth that she *could* handle it. She had done it before; she could do it again. So the relief didn't come from her never feeling anxious again; the relief came from realizing that if she did feel anxious, she could handle it. You know what happened next? Her anxiety dissipated—not because she found a way to control it, but because she addressed the fear beneath it. She understood she could make it through even if feeling anxious.

Your Body and Anxiety: It's Not All in Your Head

Anxiety can live in your body without being attached to specific thoughts. It is like an alarm going off for no obvious reason. Some bodies, for any number of historical reasons, from an acute trauma to a highly critical upbringing, can carry alarms. Why? Because your body remembers.[6] You may wake up or go to bed with this feeling. Or you may get this feeling at random moments when there's nothing specific you're anxious about. That is because our bodies hold this alarm inside it, even though there may be no words to explain it.[7]

Clients often rack their brains trying to figure out why they're feeling anxious. As they dig for the cause, they often end up feeling, well, more anxious. Sometimes there is absolutely a direct trigger for feeling anxious. Sometimes, though, it is just an old alarm in your body. We often can't help ourselves, because we've been taught that the way to calm anxiety is to control our thoughts.

Your body may sound an alarm. If so, pay attention to soothing your body's anxious reaction. I've witnessed clients turn the corner on anxiety by learning to quiet their alarms. The first step in doing that is to realize that sometimes it isn't in your head; sometimes it's in your body. Once you recognize this, you can begin to take steps to address the alarm. The tools in Chapter 5, such as breathing exercises and grounding practices, are all helpful for calming an alarm in your body.

The Predictability Under Anxiety: "Right on Time"

There is an underlying fear that accompanies an acute experience of anxiety: *What if it comes back?* I saw an increase in anxiety during the COVID-19 pandemic. I had many clients experiencing a type of anxiety they never had before. It was unsettling. They wondered, *Who is this strange new visitor, and how do I make it go away?* The tendency, which is totally understandable, is to try to stop anxiety: to block the thoughts or to shrink your world so that you never encounter that feeling again. Something, anything. Those are not the answer.

The answer to the fear *what if it comes back?* is:

It will.

But naming this predictability can bring freedom from that fear.

Years ago, when I saw Dr. Barnes, the possibility of having another anxious or scary thought was paralyzing. As I explained how terrifying this was, he patiently and attentively listened. Then he looked at me kindly, tapped his watch, and said, "When that thought comes, you just look at your watch, tap it, and say: 'Right on time.'"

The simplicity of this has stayed with me and never failed to help. What he modeled for me was that *a thought is just a thought*, and *an anxious feeling is just an anxious feeling*. It won't be the end of you. And when you take the power back from it by lightheartedly mocking its predictable return, it is a lot less alarming.

So what is underneath *your* anxiety? That is a good place to look for clues. Is it an old alarm? A fear that you can't handle it? A vulnerable feeling? A predictable pattern you can tap your watch about?

Approaching yourself when you're anxious is like taking the hand of a child and helping them turn on the light before bed. Yes, the thing they're fearing is frightening, that is, if it were real. But in the light, those scary shadows are dispelled. You both can look in the closet and underneath the bed, assuring the child that what is there is much less scary than the thing they feared.

CHAPTER 11

THE PAINFUL "WHY" OF BOUNDARY ISSUES

*"If no one has ever told you, your freedom
is more important than their anger."*

NAYYIRAH WAHEED

client, exhausted and defeated, tells me in a quiet
voice that she just doesn't know what to do anymore.
She. Just. Can't. It's all too much. She feels uncomfortable in her own skin, has "no motivation," and is tired all
the time.

"Am I depressed?" she asks me. "Maybe it's my
thyroid."

We start with listening and validating. The best places

to start. She feels awful; we meet her there with compassion. Tears stream down her face.

"But what is it?" she asks. "What is wrong with me? I have everything I need, so why do I feel like this?"

"I don't know," I tell her, "but I know the answer is in here somewhere."

We get curious. Naming pain accurately always includes a suspension of judgment. We keep talking, and some details spill out. The caretaking of a sick neighbor. The hauling around of her sons to their four different sports. Yes, four. The impossible and never-ending deadlines at work. The shockingly unhelpful husband. The mom who calls every day to vent. The trips to dialysis with her dad. It's teacher appreciation week, too, and she's in charge of it—for the *whole* school. And don't forget, she's hosting book club again this month, because no one else volunteered.

The clues begin to make sense. *Is she really unmotivated?* I wonder. *Or is she completely burned out?*

We keep listening, and a theme emerges.

"I just don't feel right telling them no."

Ah, okay. Here we are. She may feel down and unmotivated, but the arrows are pointing to exhaustion from over-giving without relief. The impact is cumulative. Some of the things can't be helped, like her dad on dialysis, but some of them *have* to go. Mom's vent sessions and hosting the book club? On the chopping block.

Someone might scold her for her lack of boundaries, but what would that solve? Instead, we find the pain in her life that is tied to her difficulty saying no. But we can't stop there. We have to ask why: Why is it hard for her to say no?

In naming this painful "why," we get somewhere. While growing up, she had never felt important in her family. Her older brother was alternately the star of the family and the nemesis. Either way, *he* got all the attention. She learned to have a place by being the pleasing one who cleaned up after dinner while her parents argued with him. And she learned to say it was no big deal when they left her gymnastics meet early to be there for his big football debut.

School wasn't easy, either. Introverted and sensitive, she didn't find a kindred spirit in her school, and so she became the "yes" girl, always helping with their homework, always sharing the favorite part of her lunch. This led to doing their homework in high school and driving drunk classmates around to parties on the weekend. She did what she knew to do to be loved. And she never outgrew it. So many of us do the same thing, don't we? The details of our stories may differ, but the motivation is the same.

She picked a husband who mimicked the patterns of

her parents. He seemed incapable of even the bare minimum of helpfulness. She grew up to repeat these behaviors in her adult life. Underneath it all was the pain of a little kid just wanting to be seen and loved. The pain in her life today, caused by a lack of boundaries, stems from a historical painful *why*. She never experienced a different way to get love.

Underneath most boundary issues are people who just want to be loved.

The Wrong Focus

Boundaries are an underdiagnosed cause of pain. That pain is usually connected to a why from your story. We too often have the wrong focus.

I was drying my hair when it hit me. Standing in my bathroom for a rare moment alone, I surveyed the last two weeks. I barely recognized myself in my exhaustion and irritability. I had given way past my boundaries. I had done everything I could to make the best experience possible, and you know what? People were still themselves. And those relationships that were supposed to get better by me creating the perfect setting? They didn't. Everyone I worked so hard to please just kind of took it. And continued to take it. Have you experienced a version of this in your own relationships?

I used to think I would get some kind of prize, or at

least an acknowledgment, for giving past my boundaries. But no. I would over-give until I resented everyone. I realized in the bathroom the people I had over-given to were not handing out prizes. It turns out that the only prize for over-giving is exhaustion, along with an expectation from others to keep it up. Can you relate?

I had read enough books; I should've known better! It didn't help to scold myself, either. Instead, I needed to uncover the "why" under my over-giving. There was a pain I was avoiding by over-giving. What was it?

I feared disapproval and rejection if I gave within my limits.

Too often we talk about boundary issues like they are just failures on the part of the boundary setter to speak up for herself, either to get her needs met or to ask for what *she* wants. So what's *really* going on?

People don't have boundary issues because they want to. Why would anyone choose the irritability, chaos, and exhaustion of a life without good boundaries? People have boundary issues because at some point they needed to. They learned that a way to protect themselves from more pain was to sacrifice themselves for the needs of others.

Laying the Groundwork First

Before we go any further, let's make sure we're on the same page. A boundary is the place where you end and others begin. It's a fence line between what you *are* responsible for and what you *aren't*. It's what you'll say yes or no to, with regard to your time, emotions, relationship, and your body.

Healthy boundaries must be flexible enough to let the good stuff in, but firm enough to keep the harmful stuff out. When our boundaries are healthy, they are flexible and sustainable, allowing us to feel more balanced. When our boundaries are too porous, we feel more chaos and more out of control. What is within your boundaries is what you're in charge of: like brushing your own teeth, paying your bills, taking care of your own children (excluding times of crisis, of course).

Pain in this area is layered. There is a reason you have fragmented boundaries, along with the painful consequences of living with them.

Let's start there, with what it feels like when your boundaries are not working.

The Wrong Yard

Your boundaries are like a fenced-in backyard. Imagine a picket fence surrounding your lovely, green lawn. What is inside your fence is your responsibility. You water it, you pull the weeds, seed it. But what if you took your hose and spent most of your time watering your neighbor's lawn? Fully convinced this is admirable, you water, weed, and seed your neighbor's lawn. You do this so much that you begin to neglect your own. There are, after all, only so many hours in the day. Without being watered, your lovely, green grass withers and dies. But your neighbor's lawn? The one you spent all your time tending? Gorgeous.

Whether it is your lawn or your life, assuming the responsibilities of others will leave your space dry and parched.[1] There are painful consequences to tending the wrong yard. Here are just a few I see in my therapy office.

Exhaustion: A common trait among people with insufficient boundaries is exhaustion. When I see a client always exhausted, I wonder with them out loud about their boundaries (this excludes those who are in a health crisis, are new parents, care-givers of someone ill, or experiencing some physical ailment). If, in the normal routine of life, they can't catch their breath, it's often because there's no time to catch it. If exhaustion is your constant companion, it doesn't mean you are doing anything wrong. But it might indicate that you could benefit from saying no more often.

Resentment: Another common theme is resentment. Resentment is a sign of giving past your boundaries. It's the warning light on the dash-board. Most definitions agree that resentment is a negative response to being mistreated.[2] You're often pissed, at all of them. Are you being mis-treated? Or are you allowing others to take advantage of your over-giving? We can feel mis-treated by doing too much. Resentment is a sim-mering irritability. When something is being kept warm on the stove, it is kept at a low tem-perature. If the heat is turned higher, little bub-bles pop up. And before you know it, resentment from poor boundaries turns a simmering resent-ment into a seething one... until you finally boil over.

A Life on Hold: Finally, with fragmented bound-aries I often see a life on hold. Whose life? *Yours.* Does that strike a chord? What are the things you wish you could get to, or even have time to think about? Caveat: A therapist once told me I could paint, write, exercise, and work with three young children at home, a husband who traveled, and running my own business. I was unfulfilled, she said, because I wasn't trying hard enough. Well, she was wrong. I *couldn't* do it all. I stopped seeing her, but I learned a valuable lesson. Since then, I am always careful to include context in any boundary discussion. You may *not* have extra time. You may be a single parent or a caretaker of a disabled spouse. If so, this section is not for you. I am referring here to those of us that do have extra time, however scant, and you're giving it to other people. The water is only going to *their* lawn. The consequence is that your dreams, goals, ideas, passions, hobbies, and interests all get put on hold. And what happens when you are walking through life with important parts of who you are perpetually on hold? It is a recipe for resentment, depression, anxiety, and burnout.

You deserve to explore *all* the parts of who you are, so let's look at the painful why underneath those fragmented boundaries.

The Painful Why

Present-day boundary issues are often historical in their roots. That is why the story of your past is so critical. Somewhere along the way you learned it was better to do exactly what your mom wanted, whether it was unreasonable or unattainable, because her cold shoulder was soul crushing. You learned to be quiet, even when laughing, whenever your dad was in *that* mood. You learned to be a parent when your parents weren't, when they were working too much, drinking too much, emotionally absent, or all of the above. You learned to sacrifice your sense of self to belong to that group at school, because the pain of being ostracized for one more year was too much. In order to fit in, you learned to assimilate, denying parts of you that you feared would be rejected. You learned to act, talk, communicate, and cower as if everyone else were smarter than you to avoid their ruthless mocking. You learned that the whole of you is to be dimmed, diminished, or denied in order to keep relationships. And so you learned *not* to set boundaries, just to make it through another school year.

Underneath many of these lesser pains is the greater pain of being unloved or alone. This pain hurts so much that we betray our own needs in order to avoid it. This is how boundary issues develop. We learn what we need to do, be, or say to stay okay with others.

When we have poor boundaries, we're often looking to create a sense of emotional safety.[3]

You may not know how to define safety, but I bet your body does. From polyvagal theory, created by Stephen Porges, and commonly referred to as "the science of feeling safe," we learn the necessity of your body feeling safe and secure with others in order to function well, heal, and engage. Safety is sensing that another person is not a threat. Our nervous system reads "safe" or "unsafe" in the physiology of another's face, often from the look in their eyes and the tone of their voice.[4] This is a subconscious reaction, and we may have a pleasing response without even consciously processing the information, especially if this is what we learned to do growing up. For some of you, it was a survival skill. Think about how our bodies react to a bear, as we discussed earlier. Now imagine this in relationships. Your desire to please and your reticence to set boundaries could be rooted in the old pain of not feeling safe.

For some, this difficulty in saying no may be evidence of a "fawn" response. We learned about fight, flight, and freeze, but according to therapist and author Pete Walker there is a fourth response in which the person who feels threatened makes themselves more pleasing so as to neutralize the threat.[5] Walker explains, "Fawn types seek safety by merging with the wishes, needs, and demands of others. They act as if they unconsciously believe that the price of admission to any relationship is the forfeiture of all their needs, rights, preferences, and boundaries."[6] An early learned behavior pattern created out of necessity to feel safe by fawning may be at play in your difficulty saying no today.

In contrast to these formative experiences, safe

relationships don't require you to push past your boundaries. These people fully embrace who you are, regardless of whatever you say yes and no to. Your body will feel safe with them.

Another way to understand the painful why under boundary issues is through attachment theory. Remember, we defined secure attachment as a parent who is able to be warm, responsive, and dependable: not perfect but tuned in to you. However, another marker of secure attachment is when children feel the freedom to share negative emotions and thoughts with their caregiver without the fear of being met with rejection, shame, or scolding.[7]

Imagine how different you might be with boundaries today if you had been allowed to express negative emotions and still feel loved. How much pleasing behavior, and therefore poor boundaries, can be traced back to this?

From where I sit in my therapist office?

A lot.

Your Why Is Your Way Out

Next time, before you scold yourself for over-giving, practice naming your pain by getting compassionately curious about your why. Naming this pain is the key to unlocking the door to doing life differently. When you learn to name the why under your boundary choices, you learn to listen to what you need. From there, start honoring your limits by setting new boundaries.

You were not meant to sacrifice yourself to be loved. It may be what you needed to do then, but that is not where you have to stay. That is not love. It is a lopsided transaction with you on the losing end.

Having boundaries is refusing to live with that imbalance any longer. Love doesn't ask you to sacrifice yourself in a way that doesn't honor your full humanity. It is refusing to leave yourself anymore. It's seeing yourself in the past, giving everything away, not in a selfless way, but in order to survive. It's taking yourself gently by the hand and saying, "I understand. You needed to give everything away to feel safe, to feel okay. It made sense then. But that's over now."

CHAPTER 12

THIS IS TOO MUCH

*"If we do not transform our pain, we
will most assuredly transmit it."*

Richard Rohr

I stopped at HomeGoods one day on the way home from work and perused the fall decor. Just a regular day. I was happy to have a moment to myself.

My phone lit up: "mommy. there's a lockdown. mama."

My oldest child at school, terrified, texted me from inside a classroom as the police were called. She was in a closet. The administrator told everyone to take shelter immediately: An active shooter was in the building.

They were trying to lock the door, but they couldn't figure out how. Children were scrambling in terror. Just children.

Their terror became mine. With my hands shaking, I typed, "Do what the teachers say. I love you."

I sat on the edge of a nearby chair. Just the week before, a loaded gun had been found by the metal detectors on her campus. The week before that, someone was murdered at the University of North Carolina at Chapel Hill, as well as several people murdered in a racist hate crime in Florida.[1]

The store felt strange now. My cart, with its fall wreath, suddenly was meaningless. I waited to hear if my daughter was okay, wondering if I would ever hear from her again. I wondered if her school was okay.

It turned out to be a drill. Her class didn't know because they had a substitute who hadn't been informed.

When I finally got to my car, I cried. I felt so much fear, so much rage. I cried that this is our reality. A threat like this is possible at any moment in our country, and we can't seem to change it. I cried for every parent whose child *wasn't* okay, when it *wasn't* a drill. And this was just an ordinary afternoon at HomeGoods in a very privileged life.

So far, we have named a lot of historical pains, along with some in the present. But what about the pain of just living in this world? It can feel like an exposed nerve, feelings raw and the emotional pain excruciating.

A client plops on my couch. "I don't know what's wrong with me. I'm so anxious this week." She rattled off current events that had her worried, which were not connected to her anxiety. Her knee-jerk reaction was to blame herself. Surely the cause for her increased anxiety was her fault. Can you see what she was doing? She was doing what we all do, underestimating the context of what she is living in.

It can feel like being a fish living in an aquarium that never gets cleaned out. Green algae grows in it. The water is cloudy, so the visibility goes down. And the oxygen level goes down with it. That's the environment we live in, where we swim around unable to see, unable to breathe, feeling awful, and wondering, "What's wrong with me today?"

I stayed curious with my client. "Tell me more about what you were just listening to in the car." It was a regular weekly podcast, she told me. It was about injustices and crises that should bring us all to our knees. As she listed them to me, becoming more upset, the connection dawned on her. Her feelings suddenly made sense. She was surprised at first when I asked her more about the podcast. She had learned, like so many of us have, that our feelings should be independent of our environment. This is not only inaccurate, it's impossible. Our feelings are never independent of our environment.

This whole world, *all this out here* (imagine me waving my hands) is a lot. Many of you readers live in the United States, and as I write, there are mass shootings, school shootings, hate crimes, books being banned. And that is just what makes the news. It is not even touching on the historical traumas and injustices. There are food insecurity, poverty, racism, police brutality, domestic violence, and people facing homelessness. The environment is quaking. Perhaps you can't stand your in-laws. Maybe your boss is demeaning. The list goes on.

Not only the events in your own world but also in the whole world *impact you*. What I don't see us naming enough in regard to pain is acknowledging that this is a lot. *Everything* outside of you is impacting you, *every day*. The impact will be different for each of us based on many factors, including our individual stories, histories, privileges, or lack thereof. It's certainly not all the same. Our experiences are not all equal. But we're expected to walk out into this world as if it's all normal. This is not normal, and it's definitely not okay.

You may be anxious because truly anxiety-provoking things are happening all around you. But if you don't understand that, you might be hard on yourself for how you feel. You may be struggling with depression that is based on what it is like to be you in the world. We don't talk about that enough, either. We have to name what is happening in the world around us in order to understand ourselves in it. We must acknowledge the micro and macro in order to find accurate understanding. You may be living in an environment in a large sense or in your home in a smaller sense, both of which may be toxic. Contextualizing this helps to make sense of it. You can't name that pain if you *don't* consider your environment. Instead, we too often blame the person who is struggling.

Your Feelings Are Reasonable

I would like to walk around with a pin to hand out to people. It would simply say, "You make sense."

I can't tell you how many times I've sat with an insightful, self-aware client during a crisis in their life, their community, in their country, or in the world, and said to them, "No, you are *not* overreacting; your feelings make sense. If your heart is heavy, this means you're paying attention."

They may be criticized for being dramatic. Maybe they were told they *always* overreact. They may have a partner who is "always calm," or just be ingesting messages from society at large. There are a lot of sources that can shame you into thinking you feel too much or that you are making too much of something by having those feelings.

You're anxious when a war breaks out, for example. That's reasonable.

You're scared when children get shot in schools—reasonable.

You're outraged when injustices happen—reasonable.

You're terrified when there is another hate crime on the news—reasonable.

You're heartbroken for your friend from college who just lost her baby—reasonable.

The list goes on. Having constant access to the pains and injustices happening every day in the world via technology in the palm of your hand can feel paralyzing. That's because our coping has not caught up to our access. It is impacting all of us, all the time. The suffering of another human *should* impact us—always.

But we are not equipped to know how to carry so many things, especially tragic things, all at once. The result? Most of us feel overwhelmed. It's okay to feel this way. It makes sense to feel this way. *You* are not too much, *this* is too much.

You make sense.

There's Something in the Air

When I was newly married, we lived in a 1940s bungalow in an industrial part of the city. It had a great little front porch with a wooden swing. It was surrounded by train tracks, warehouses, and a giant gray hill. This hill was created by a quarry, grinding through rocks. Whenever the wind blew, so would the gray, pulverized rock. Some days, you could see it billowing in a gust of air. Other days, as I wiped it off the front porch, I thought in horror, *I am inhaling this every day.*

Some neighbors led a charge to hold the owners accountable and fix the problem, but the owners of the quarry denied the severity of the problem. As I looked at the gray covering my front porch and swing, I wondered how they could deny what we all could see. Then I realized, it's there, but it is in their best interest to deny it.

When there's something in the air, it permeates everything. What we touch, what we eat, what we drink. It's what we live in, raise babies in, fall in love in, get hurt in. When something is in the air, you might be told, "There's nothing there, stop overreacting, it's all in your imagination, I'm not bothered, I don't notice anything." It's often those not impacted who deny its existence. It's often those believing they will never be impacted who insist, just like the owners of that gray hill, "It's all good! The air is fine!"

As a therapist, my job is to visit places I have not lived in order to witness, honor, and name. Therefore, I could not write a book on pain without addressing the systemic things that plague our society and hurt people. I am not an expert on the experience of the many types of pain caused by these systems of oppression or these societal toxins in the air. I don't know what pains of living in this world impact you, but my work would be incomplete without including them.

Pain is not just an individual experience. It is also a larger, systemic, oppressive presence in the world. It comes in many forms: racial oppression, gender inequality, injustice, mass incarceration, misogyny, homophobia, transphobia, ableism, xenophobia, violence, war and more. It doesn't feel right to simply list these pains, because each one is a world unto itself. But it's important to understand their roots are deep, spanning generations that have carried these pains to the present day.

It's All Connected

Our experience in this world is like a set of concentric circles. There you are in the middle, doing your best. In your circle is your genetic makeup, your unique story, all the pains you are able to name, and all the beauty of who you were made to be. Then there is your immediate circle, your family, whatever the makeup. Then friends, then coworkers, then your neighborhood, your city. The circles keep getting larger, encompassing more of the world, along with its problems. On any given day that little you in the middle may be feeling the weight of those concentric circles.

This helps to explain that you are not just upset that you forgot the milk at the store. Experiences like that happen in a larger context. Maybe you are feeling weighed down from a number of circles that day...and it all gets pinned on the milk.

No matter how you and I may differ in our experiences, there is one thing I wish I could shout from the rooftops: Everything is connected! *Everything.* Meaning, everything you experience in the world impacts everything inside you. All those concentric circles are connected, and they are all connected *to you.* And so, when you are angry about the milk, get curious. Can you imagine how much more compassion you would have for yourself if you addressed how you are feeling based on everything you've experienced in your body, community, and history each day?

It is essential you understand that often your hard day, your depression, your anxiety, your anger can be directly related to what it's like to be you in the world, in all its interconnected ways. Without that information, it's easy to reduce your pain to surface symptoms rather than the complex interaction of causes.

Finally, sometimes the circles of your personal life hold an awful lot. Someone has an unsettling diagnosis. Maybe *you* are that someone. You might be a caregiver of a baby or multiple young children, an aging parent, or all of the above. Maybe your partner lost their job, maybe you lost yours. What I see over and over again is that the most thoughtful, intentional people are often the hardest on themselves when things are just, well, hard. You may be doing everything right, and it's still a lot. And hard. And overwhelming. Saying this allows you to avoid the tendency to fault yourself.

Some of the biggest relief I see happen is when a client and I name together: "This is just really hard; you're not doing anything wrong. It's all connected. And it's a lot in your circles right now." Often, a predictable exhale occurs when the narrative shifts from "Why am I having such a hard time? What is wrong with me?" to "This is exactly why I am having a hard time." In that exhale of understanding, there is often a gentleness with ourselves that didn't exist before.

Why do I ask you to validate every concentric circle of what it is like to be you in the world? Put simply: It's one of the best ways to love yourself.[2] Love never denies the pain. Love sees it, seeks to understand it. Love is big enough for all the circles. And moving from there, you will not only be more kind to yourself, you will better understand what you need.

Keep Your Tender Heart

Tenderness is required to name the pain of living in this world. It is one of our greatest defenses against all pain. In my opinion, change in this world happens because of hearts that are open to their own pain—and to the pain of others. This helps us to "transform our pain, not transmit it," as Richard Rohr writes.[3] Tenderness refuses to shut down. It refuses to deny anyone's humanity. It moves from there into action. It also names pain in order not to pass it on. You keep your heart tender by not hardening it to the world and by not denying the pain of being in the world for yourself and for others. Tenderness is one of our greatest resources. The more we give it to ourselves, the more we are able to give it to others.[4]

This is all a lot, I know. Shutting down your heart is one way to deal with it. But there is a better way, a gentler way. Naming the pain with tenderness honors your pain. Knowing the impact of those concentric circles doesn't solve your pain, but it helps you to more accurately name what you are carrying, to assess what you need going forward, and to ask yourself where you can be a part of change.

CHAPTER 13

WHAT WAS YOUR CREATIVE STRATEGY?

"I have woven a parachute out of everything broken..."
WILLIAM STAFFORD

Tenderness is required in naming any pain. It's also what we need for this part of the journey.

We have practiced naming pain, but we also need to look backward. Before you had a name for it, what did you do with that unnamed pain? How did you, and how do you, typically cope with it?

We all develop coping strategies as children to deal with hard things. For example, you may have learned to be the funniest in the room to get attention. Perhaps you learned to deny your needs to avoid stressing out your mom. Maybe you made sure to have everything perfect to avoid getting yelled at by your dad.

Though we often don't recognize it, these are all creative strategies. In therapy I often find myself saying to adult clients, in reflecting on their childhood, "Wow, that was such a creative strategy you figured out in order to survive." They may be discussing something in marriage therapy that's hard, or they may be regretting a pattern of frustrating behavior. But when we get curious, without judgment, we can usually trace this behavior back to a strategy that was developed early on to make it through something. And it was pretty smart, at the time. The same is likely true for you.

We have all adjusted in some way to make it to today. Many of the ways we behave today are actually adaptations. This news should foster self-compassion. Don't like the way you do something? Wonder why you're always so anxious? Why do you shut down when people have big feelings? Why is it hard for you to trust a good moment? Get curious, really curious. It's likely these are adaptations you developed that were necessary for you to make it through a difficult season.

We were coping in these ways because we didn't know what else to do with our pain. The coping might have created additional pain, but it existed because it was the only way we knew how to handle the pain we were in.

When clients understand that their responses of anxiety, depression, and numbing helped them to cope, they are more likely to feel more empowered and more self-compassion. For example, research demonstrates that clients who were taught that PTSD was an understandable response to what they'd been through, rather than a terrible disorder, had better outcomes in treatment. Similarly, clients who were taught that their stress reactions were positive and could help them overcome challenges experienced more courage and joy rather than fear.

How we label our behaviors matters. The ways that you learned to cope were necessary. Trauma therapist Courtney Armstrong summarizes this truth by referring to symptoms as "allies." They were, and are, trying to help you.[1]

It must be added that I am in no way minimizing the destructive qualities any type of coping may have on you or on other people in your life. I'm suggesting instead that you learn better ways to cope by understanding yourself and, if applicable, forgiving yourself for the ways you coped when you knew no other options. Now that you are learning how to name your pain, you have other options.

Maya Angelou has famously said, "Do the best you can until you know better. Then, when you know better, do better."

The Strategies You Outgrow

Imagine trying on a T-shirt from when you were eight years old. It's no longer your size, but it once fit perfectly. You can barely get your head through the hole. And the arms? Impossible. There's no denying this shirt no longer fits you.

We often walk around using strategies for coping with pain that once fit but don't anymore. Let's expand on some of the ideas we touched on briefly in Chapter 6 about coping in the family you grew up in.

I sat with a client who learned to get as small as she possibly could to avoid being criticized. It started with constant yelling and blaming from both her parents. They seemed to take turns. As a result, she stopped raising her hand in class, even when she knew the answer. Like a duckling, she followed anyone who told her to do anything. She became so deeply buried inside herself that it was unclear if she was still in there. When I met her she was deeply depressed, confused, and had no idea what she wanted or even how to know what she wanted.

"People say, 'Just be yourself,'" she told me, "but I have no idea who that is."

Anything that didn't live up to her narcissistic parents' expectations became another threat of their shaming. Any need she had that didn't fit into their plans was more reason to humiliate her. She became so withdrawn that she was like a shadow that skirted down the walls of their house, slinking back into her room after foraging through the fridge for something to eat. To survive that environment, she *needed* to disappear.

Now that she is an adult, this strategy doesn't fit anymore. But she had no idea how to move from translucent to opaque, from a shadow to a whole person. She genuinely thought this *was* her personality. But it was her way of coping that needed to disappear, not her.

Sometimes our ways of coping are hurtful, not only to ourselves but to those around us. I sat with a different client, fresh from couples therapy with another therapist. She told me her partner was exhausted by her rigid perfectionism and constant criticism. She cried as she recounted the terror she felt whenever her mother arrived home, fearing her mother's angry withdrawal when she didn't measure up. This cycle of anger and withdrawal took its toll.

"It was never good enough," she stated matter-of-factly. "*I* was never good enough." In her mind, it was as settled an assumption as the law of gravity.

And now? Now she is never good enough *for herself*. "I

just can't stop. I don't want to be obsessed with the house, but I don't know how to rest. It makes me anxious. I'm always exhausted." Her greatest grief, though, is how hard she is on her partner and kids. "I know I'm hurting them. I see it. I always promise myself I won't do it again. Then I do," she grieved, her voice heavy with regret.

Why is she doing something she regrets?

Because her coping in childhood has not caught up to her adult life.

She learned early to be as perfect as she could to avoid her mother's anger and her constant rebukes. But it came at a cost.

She internalized this coping. A deep fear rooted itself in her of ever being anything but "the best," or anyone she loved ever being anything but the best. Growing up, she drove herself to perfection to protect herself. But that strategy no longer served her. In fact, it hurt her and the people she loves.

This is important to understand: *She is not a perfectionist, she's afraid.*

We start to find her way home by learning to identify these behaviors with compassion, understanding, and forgiveness. She needed the strategy then; now she needs to let it go.

In her defense, she did what she needed to do to be loved.

How about you? What did *you* have to do to be loved?

There may be someone specific, or perhaps several someones, who come to mind when you think about adapting in order to be loved. This may be a parent, grandparent, a sibling, a friend, an early romantic relationship. Likely it's a person you have some history with.

The thing for us to know about these patterns is that we often globalize them.[2] We follow the same rules we learned in foundational relationships, and we apply them to other relationships. It is the way our brains work to protect us.[3] Imagine if you burned your hand on a stove you didn't know was hot. Your hand may instinctively retreat each time you are near a stove again. The stove may not even be hot, but your hand remembers.

Think again about that T-shirt you wore as a child. It may have fit perfectly when you were little, but it wouldn't fit now, right?

Your creative strategy is the same.

Shedding your strategies is a molting process, like shedding old feathers. Your old covering was necessary before, but it doesn't fit anymore. We shed these strategies by approaching them from our adult selves, naming the pain that created them, understanding them, then thanking them for protecting us.

Part of that shedding is naming not just your pain but

also your strategies. Creative strategies you once needed turn into coping patterns you use today.

Let's take a closer look at them.

What's Your Coping Style?

None of us arrived to adulthood without pain. Consequently, we came up with strategies to deal with it. Therapist, professor, author, and creator of restoration therapy Dr. Terry Hargrave gives an organizing map of different types of coping behaviors that are typically developed with the different kinds of pains we all experience.

You may have experienced some sort of wound that correlated with your identity, by how you were or weren't loved. Or your sense of safety, by how much trust you felt you could place in others. Or both. We come into this world asking two questions: *Am I loved?* and *Am I safe?* These are never answered perfectly. But when the answers are no, the pain can be so excruciating that somehow we have to find a way to cope.[4]

These are some common ways of coping, according to Hargrave:[5]

> *Blame and Shame:* Blaming includes behaviors like criticizing, critiquing others, anger, and rage. It is taking the pain you feel and finding

something to blame in other people, which is the fight response of fight or flight.

If blame moves outward, shame moves inward, more like the flight or freeze responses. This is criticizing and shaming yourself as a way of coping with the pain. Because the self cannot bear the weight of these self-inflicted attacks, your sense of self often collapses in on itself.

Controlling and Escape/Chaos: Controlling behaviors may be related to you or to others. This style is also more of a fight response. People who have become controlling in order to cope often feel the need to be flawless in order to avoid judgment or criticism, which is at the heart of perfectionism. You control to feel safe.

Those who cope with escape and chaos, which is more of a flight or freeze response, might have addictive behaviors like substance abuse or overspending. They try to escape their feelings by numbing them or by creating chaos in their lives to distract them. They might withdraw, even to the point of dissociation.

Do you see your own ways of coping in these examples?

Naming our coping behaviors helps us better understand our story. We contextualize our behaviors when we see them as ways of coping with pain. When we see *why* we have developed these ways of coping, our life begins to make more sense. As a result, we become more compassionate with ourselves.

This Is Not Who You Are

We don't simply lose ourselves in unnamed pain; we lose ourselves in unrecognized coping.

That is, until we learn a better way.

One of my favorite movies is *Moana*, in large part because of one scene that depicts a truth better than words could ever describe it.[6] At the end of the film, the young Moana has been commissioned to return the heart to Te Fiti, a goddess whose heart had been stolen. Because of the theft, the world has been slowly dying, all plant life withering away.

The goddess's heart is a green stone that Moana holds in her hand, an island away.

But the terrifying monster, Te Kā, is blocking her path. The monster's form is cracked rock, beneath which is molten lava. Seeing Moana, it rages at her from the barren island it inhabits.

Undeterred, the courageous girl steps into the ocean that separates them. As she does, the water parts, creating a path for her. Moana walks slowly, deliberately, softly singing as she approaches the enraged monster.

As Moana nears, she compassionately speaks truth to the monster: "This is not who you are." This slows the monster's menacing approach. As it listens, she speaks: "You know who you are, who you *truly* are."

Te Kā bends down, her face now inches from Moana's. The brave girl lifts her head higher. They connect, touching foreheads and noses.

Moana returns the heart to Te Kā, placing it in a spot covered in hardened lava. Suddenly, Te Kā begins to transform. The lava cools to rock. The rock cracks open. And the beautiful green goddess, Te Fiti, emerges from within the shell, her head adorned with flowers, her locks flowing with vines. As her hand touches the rock-encrusted surface beneath her, lush greenery spreads from her. Not only is Te Kā transformed but so is everything around her.

In all her pain, the beautiful, life-giving Te Fiti had become the terrifying, life-destroying Te Kā. Her way of coping was with rage and fury.

But her true self was still in there, still beautiful and still full of life.

So is yours.

We all become a version of Te Kā when our hearts are stolen by pain. We forget our true name. We can become unrecognizable in our coping.

Are these ways of coping masking your true self?

If so, let me tell you as gently and compassionately as I can...

That is *not* who you are.

PART 3

THE RETURNING–
YOU ARE NOT YOUR PAIN

CHAPTER 14

WHAT'S THE STORY YOU'VE BEEN BELIEVING?

"Don't turn away. Keep your gaze on the bandaged place. That's where the light enters you."

Rumi

This is the part of the book where I am supposed to give you The Solution. I am supposed to reveal one thing that no one else knows. *Surprise.* Here it is, the secret to healing all your pains and solving all your problems.

But I don't have any secret. And I am suspicious of those who say they do.

Years ago, I heard a popular author teach that a book

161

should present a problem and then solve it. Although in some cases this can be a helpful model, it is often misused. It can be manipulative to promise that a book can solve hard things. It is at least misleading; at worst, it is dishonest.

As a therapist, I don't believe in quick fixes. I sit up close with real pain. My clients and I clean up the messes that such promises have created. Real life is too complex for simple solutions. These gimmicks are not only useless, they're harmful, especially when they leave a hurting person believing that *they* are the reason it didn't work.

Books and therapy are only tools. Effective tools, hopefully, but not the answer to life. They are not powerful enough to be that.

At the end of particularly intense sessions with clients, I often find myself saying something like, "There is unfortunately no bow to wrap this up with." We may exchange a knowing laugh or a somber nod. This isn't resignation, it is validation.

After this admission I hope they are left with what I want to tell you: Your pain is too sacred for a simple solution. Your story is too complex. And you matter too much to have your hurts reduced to platitudes.

So we won't.

Instead, we will sit together in the complexity of

your story. We will walk toward your pain, into it and through it, and work to find understanding.

I am not bringing a Band-Aid to your wound. You deserve better than that. There will be no tidy, three-step process to solve your pain. There will certainly be no bow.

Why?

Because there is a better way.

With Yourself

In the absence of manufactured solutions, I hope you have learned to walk down the hill to yourself, to be with your pain, regardless how small it seems, or how severe.

Here is my hope as a therapist. I envision a throng of people refusing to leave themselves alone in their pain anymore, walking down the hill to themselves. This may seem a small revolution, but moving toward your pain is the embodiment of love.

Without anyone's permission, without any authority figure to validate your story, without those who hurt you to acknowledge your pain, you go. Tentatively, at first. And slowly. Then you run.

Toward the pain.

Your pain is the way home. Understand, though, that when you make it down that hill, you won't arrive with the perfect solution. You will arrive to *be with* yourself.

When I sit with someone in my office and we finally

name what they have experienced, we don't necessarily solve it. We come down the hill, refusing to misdiagnose, minimize, ignore, or look away. We draw near to the pain, and therefore near to themself.

Rewriting the Story

Your pains need your presence. They need you to bend down, stay awhile, listen, refusing to look away. Naming them will be attending to them.

However, other pains have written a false story about you. These pains need you to rewrite the story more accurately.

Imagine that when you get to the bottom of the hill, you find yourself swept up into a tornado of false narratives. In that swirling vortex of allegations, you hear that you are unlovable, perhaps, or worthless, even deserving of the pain you are experiencing.

If those are narratives you have believed, it is time to rewrite your story. We practice this by identifying what your pain has been calling you.

Years ago, my own therapist taught me that there was a step beyond naming my pain. He taught me to listen to what it had named *me*.

He called these names my "core beliefs."[1] These beliefs colored everything in my life, almost as if I were wearing a pair of dark glasses. Instead of believing that the glasses were the problem, I believed something was wrong *with me*. It never occurred to me that this story could be false. The same applies to you.

Remember Sherlocking your life? The quill pen on the table in the study does not always lie there passively, waiting to be named. It writes stories about you, stories crafted by inaccuracies. Learning to come home to who you are starts with picking up that pen and correcting your story.

As you start, remember...

You are not who the pain said you were.

The Story Your Pain Wrote

Our beliefs surrounding what has happened to us can create the most pain. If I could give you one gift, it would be to see yourself for who you truly are.

You are *not* what happened to you. You are *not* your interpretation of what happened to you. You are *not* unlovable because you weren't loved well. You are *not* defective because of what you went through. And you are *not* "other" because you weren't accepted.

Those are interpretations of your pain. Often, the shaming interpretation of any hard experience weighs us down more than the experience itself. I picture those interpretations like the old-fashioned overhead projector from my high school days. The teacher would turn off the classroom lights, turn on the machine, and start with one clear sheet, writing on it with a marker. Then she would layer another sheet on top of the first. Because of that overlay, we could no longer see the original information.

The same thing happens with our interpretations. There is the original experience, the first sheet. Layered on top of it is the interpretation we have adopted about ourselves from the experience.

These beliefs are often silent, until you learn to listen for them.[2] I ask clients to listen to what they feel when they leave a professional meeting or a social engagement that didn't go well. What runs through their mind on the way home? "I am too much"... "They will never really like me"... "I will always be on my own"... "If they only knew who I really am."

The belief pattern is there; you just have to look for it. Perhaps an illustration will help.

When I was growing up, Magic Eye posters were all the rage. They were a maze of repeating patterns, revealing nothing. But, if you cocked your head just right or gave it a side glance, a three-dimensional figure would pop out. The figure was always there, but you had to know how to look for it. The same is true of our beliefs about ourselves. They are right in front of us, but we have to learn *how* to see them.

Identifying Your Pain Narratives

Remember those questions, *Am I loved? Am I safe?* According to Dr. Hargrave, their answers inform not only our coping behaviors but also our beliefs about our identity and how safe we felt in our relationships.[3]

What are the messages *you* received about being loved?

What messages did you get from your family, friends, or teachers that were layered over your true identity, obscuring it? These can create primary emotions about how you perceive yourself. They answer the question: *Am I loved?*

The answers to that question vary with each person, but here are some of them: *unloved, unworthy, insignificant, alone, worthless, devalued, defective, inadequate, rejected, unaccepted, unwanted, abandoned, unappreciated, hopeless.*

Do you identify with any of these? What are one or two from this list that name the story that distorted how you saw your identity? Are there words not on this list that are more accurate for you?

In addition to these feelings about your identity are those about your safety in relationships. Were you able to trust people? Were your caregivers reliable? Who let you down? Who didn't protect you? What answers did you get to the question *Am I safe?*[4]

Those answers might be: *unsafe, used, fearful,*

powerless, out of control, disconnected, betrayed, insecure, unable to measure up, unknown, unsure.

What are one or two words listed that you identify with? Feel free to add your own.

Finding these words will help you understand the story you have believed about yourself. When we believe these pain narratives, we often find ourselves coping with some form of blame, shame, control issues, or escape measures. Because it is too painful to listen to these narratives, you will often move into a coping behavior instead.

For example, my narratives are "I'm somehow bad" and "I am not safe." What do I do when I feel that way? I practice a combination of shame, anxiety when I feel bad, and criticizing others when I feel unsafe. My friend's story produced feelings that sound more like "alone" and "not good enough." When she feels these things, she moves toward her anger and defensiveness.

What about you? What do *you* feel? And what do you do when you have that feeling?

Waking Up

We don't walk around looking for hurtful narratives to believe.

Unfortunately, there isn't an all-knowing narrator who tracks your story, interrupting when you are making the wrong interpretation about your painful experiences. No, instead something happens, and you conclude something. You were likely a kid when you made those conclusions, and likely alone in it. That conclusion is usually some variation of "something is wrong with me."

But what if nothing *is* wrong with you?

Learning the truth about yourself is like waking up from a bad dream. When you believe that your pain is because something is wrong with you, there's no way out. But in waking up to the truth, there is hope. Yes, maybe you are hurting, maybe you need help, or medication, or to change the choices you're making. Maybe there are things you need to do differently. Even so, you are worthy of love, you're not a mistake, not tainted, and not "other." This doesn't mean you are flawless. It means that the overarching fear that you are *all bad* is untrue.

So, let's wake up from this bad dream together.

You needed an answer for why you felt bad, and shame provided one.

But it wasn't true. Here is the truth: You're not bad. You're not a hopeless failure.

There is nothing wrong with you. There never was.

That wasn't the problem.

The problem was the problem.

It was only your conclusion about the problem that was incorrect.

Whatever breath you have been holding, you can exhale it now. This will become a lifelong practice. Although we name this today, you will return to it over and over again.

In the next chapter, we will look at returning home to the truth of who you are under the pain, under the coping, and in spite of the false narratives.

CHAPTER 15

YOU ARE NOT YOUR PAIN

"The time will come when, with elation you will greet yourself arriving at your own door, in your own mirror and each will smile at the other's welcome."

DEREK WALCOTT

We often arrive at adulthood with unexamined beliefs about ourselves—that is, until we hold them up to the light and take a better look. We believed the narratives that pain wrote because we didn't know better.

But now, we get to choose. Pain narratives lead you away from yourself with false interpretations. Choosing what to believe is coming back to the truth.

Let me illustrate. Imagine the best home you have ever known or visited. If you didn't have a loving home, imagine your ideal home. It's a place you long to return to, right? When you are away from a place you cherish, you feel homesick for that place. It offers a respite away from the rest of the world that no other place can.

You rehearse the moment of return. The welcoming sound of the door opening. The inviting place where you sit. That favorite mug. Those familiar creaks in the floor. The muffled sounds outside the windows.

Walking inside, you drop your bags as if they weighed a hundred pounds. This place, it greets you. You breathe in. There is finally relief for that ache. You are home. You exhale.

Home is not only a physical place, it is also a metaphor of who you were made to be. It is like a song your soul can only hum, because a long time ago it forgot the words. Coming home is remembering those words, realizing, possibly for the first time, that this is the place you are made to live from.

"But what kept me away so long?" you ask. "Where have I been?"

You got lost, like we all do. Like a faithful soldier following an incompetent leader who is headed in the wrong direction, you have followed your pain narratives. That is how you got lost.

But now you get to choose.

There is still a light in the window, waiting for you to

come home. The light may flicker, but it never goes out. Even if it feels like forever since you have been at home with yourself, it is there.

Even in painful times, it is still there.

Separating Who You Are from the Pain

We are often taught some version of the idea that healing is the absence of what hurts you. While there can be some truth to that, it is misleading. You may hurt while you heal. You may hurt *and* feel presence and love.

There's more freedom in separating *who you are* from the pain than in being pain free. It is separating who you are from having to be symptom free, who you are from feeling great all the time. Sometimes it's just not that tidy.

Sometimes healing comes from saying, "I believe in my worth, even in this struggle, even if *I* struggle."

That kind of healing reorders how you view yourself. It roots you deeper than whatever winds of pain blow your way and threaten to uproot you. Your worth is inherent, and it was always there, underneath everything.

Identifying the truth of who you are has more nuance than just "the real you." People often get overwhelmed by that idea, understandably so. Some things change us, some things try to change us but fail, and some parts of us have always been there and are waiting for us to rediscover them.

This is the exhale of choosing the truth. It isn't a motivational speech. It's finding more air to breathe. It feels like relief, like returning, like coming home, like remembering the lyrics you have forgotten.

There are different ways to conceptualize who you are, apart from your pain. Here are a few of them:

Who You Are Underneath: Think about the you that first existed underneath all those transparencies that were scribbled on by your pain, overlaying the original one on the overhead projector. You know, the ones that have been put on the screen for everyone to see. That overlay of narratives may have obscured your worth, but it can't erase it. Removing those overlays, one by one, will reveal the *real* you underneath.

The pain you experienced historically can also feel like a weight on your chest. It's not uncommon to feel heavy with pain, depression, anxiety, or loss.[1] But you are *not that weight*. The weight is valid; it hurts. Who you are is underneath that weight.

Reclaiming Who You Were Before: This process of uncovering can feel like getting reacquainted with younger parts of yourself.[2] Maybe this idea feels new to you, but many therapy models agree that our younger selves are still inside us. Reclaiming earlier versions of yourself doesn't mean regressing. It means holding the hand of the younger you that was hurt, revisiting, nurturing, and reclaiming those parts of yourself that have been taken from you by other people or by painful circumstances.

Who You Became Despite the Pain: Resilience can be defined as overcoming hardship. It involves a level of mental, emotional, and behavioral flexibility to get through difficult things.[3] It's important not only to name pain but also to realize who you have become despite the pain. For example, in working with clients whose parents didn't care well for them, we might honor the sense of capability they admire about themselves, while also honoring who they were forced to become because of the neglect.

This realization casts you as the overcomer. This allows you to honor the character that has been developed in you. It is not being dismissive or putting a silver lining around the clouds that darkened your childhood. Rather, it is honoring the breathtaking miracle of who you are today, despite who or what tried to take you out.

Eyes on the What's True

On a school field trip in fifth grade, I got to visit Washington, D.C. One of the places we toured was the government facility that printed money. Particularly mesmerizing was the machine that produced sheets of currency. As the machine whirred, the tour guide tried to get our attention for an unexpected philosophical moment. What he said stuck with me.

"You know how to tell if a hundred-dollar bill is fake?" he asked. Now we were riveted. "You stare every day at a real one, and then you will be able to spot the fakes."

Each of us has a true self, a self with inherent worth, which is undeniable, unrepeatable, and unadulterated by pain.[4] The way to recognize that worth is to stare at the real thing. The way to know the real thing is to spend time with the truth of who you are. So, when a counterfeit story circulates about who you are—and it will—you can stare it down with confidence and say, "No, that's a fake."

Every one of us is imprinted with inherent worth. Think about it like this. As I sit here, I can look down and see the pulsing of my heart in the soft place on my wrist, which happens whether or not I am attending to it. There is a life coursing through me that I did not create, cannot take credit for, which exists whether I pay attention to it or not.

The same is true about *your* inherent worth.

It exists whether you acknowledge it or not.

Finding Your Truth

Although we all share inherent worth, we often arrive at that truth differently.

What is the unique grounding truth that you can return to? What is the call from home that only you can hear, that only you can answer? It is helpful to get specific in your language. There are different ways to identify this truth. Here are a few.

> *Reparenting Yourself:* In finding language that resonates with a client, we employ the idea of reparenting their younger selves. That moment, for example, when you needed a loving adult who wasn't there for you is often when some of the pain narratives were written. But you are an adult now. You may not have had a say then, but you have a say now. If you returned to the young

person you once were, bent down, and put your arm around her...what would you say? What is it she needed to hear back then? Lean down and speak this truth to her.

I sat with a client who told her younger self that she would never leave her alone again. Another tells her younger self that everything her mom said about her wasn't true, and she is going to be okay now. Another tells himself, "You are not like your father." Another sighs emotionally as she says, "I see you, you matter, and you always did."

What God Says About You: I was trained as a therapist to follow the lead of my client when it comes to matters of faith. So if my clients want to discuss their faith, we do. If they have been wounded by a faith community, we unpack that, careful to only use language that feels safe. If they have no faith practice, we go with that. You see my point.

When it comes to finding language for the truth about who you are, many clients do turn to their faith. They turn to who God says they are and to how God loves them: a love beyond our human comprehension in its scope and reach. There is an anchoring for them that reaches down and below hurtful experiences they had with other humans. God is bigger; the truth is deeper. Their truth comes from a place that is deeper than those experiences can touch.

I will follow your lead, too. If you resonate with this, what is the truth that you hear God calling you home with? If you could hear the voice of a loving God speaking tenderly to you in those hurting spaces, what is the truth you would hear?

Who Are You on Your Best Day?: For some of you, this may all be a bit much. If the reparenting and God imagery are a bit ethereal for you, that's okay. We can meet wherever you feel most comfortable.

Another way to identify the truth of who you are, independent of the pain, is to imagine who you are on your best day. You know the one, whether it is a real experience or an imagined one. It's the day when you are believing the pure, unadulterated truth about yourself and treating yourself accordingly. Who is that person? What is the truth about her?

I always return to an example I was taught in training.[5] A woman who was deeply depressed was reminded of who she is on her best day. It turns out that same woman had previously chosen to hike and conquer an incredibly high peak. The therapist acted out this moment: hand high, foot up on the chair, just like on the summit. The client joined the therapist, acting out this truth. Her takeaway? She is still that person, no matter how she feels today.

Your Turn: What is it for you? Some truths that are grounding for many are: *loved, worthy, significant, not alone, prized, valuable, precious, adequate, approved, accepted, wanted, appreciated, free, safe, secure, sure, capable, empowered, protected, connected, competent, enough.*[6]

Do you identify with one of these, or with another word? Using the prompts and this list, reflect on the truth for you. Listen to what you hear.

What will you return to? What is the truth you hear?

Follow those truths home. The light is still in the window, awaiting your arrival.

Experiential Practice

When I first started writing, I was given this advice: "You get better at writing by writing, so write." This was not only annoying to me, it was unacceptable, because I wanted to arrive as a fully baked writer, like a beautiful pie. Instead, I arrived like an undercooked roll, doughy and needing more time in the oven.

To change metaphors, it's like being a kid who is frustrated they can't play basketball well when they've never spent time shooting baskets. Silly, right? But we do this with practicing the truth of who we are. We want to feel our worth all at once and be done with it. We want to have one insight and be a fully baked pie. But no change happens that way.

Change happens little by little. And the good news? Changing what you believe about yourself is a scientific possibility. Our brains are capable of change, which is in many ways what we experience in the process of healing. Our brains can change, adapt, and reorganize. This is called neuroplasticity.[7]

This gives hope for changing how you feel about yourself that is grounded in scientific evidence. You aren't held captive by what your brain once believed. Your story is still being written, as are narratives you embrace about who you are. We are always being re-created by what we are believing.

Healing is a practice, not a destination.

You have been practicing a way of viewing yourself through pain narratives since you can remember, likely since that event started composing them. You must also now practice believing in the value of who you are and the worth that is coursing through you. You must practice it to know it. Replace the pain narratives you identified with the truth that you are naming. When those false narratives resurface, remember the truth.

Practice living it.

And *keep* practicing.

It's Always There

In one of my favorite songs, "Rainbow" by Kacey Mus-graves, she describes a rainbow hanging above a person's head.[8] But that person doesn't know it's there. They walk around with an umbrella, unaware of the radiant beauty arching over them. Long after the rain has stopped, we still walk around with our umbrellas. Not knowing we are covered with such exquisite beauty, we miss seeing who we really are.

It is true, rainbows come from rain, but it is also true that they stay long after it stops. What is most miraculous is that they always exist within the water. The components that produce the rainbow are held within each raindrop. It is the light going into the water and out through it that produces the rainbow. The process reveals what is already there.

The same is true for you.

It isn't that pain reveals your beauty, it is that it can't stop the beauty from being revealed.

CHAPTER 16

NOTES FOR THE ROAD

"You don't think your way into a new kind of living.
You live your way into a new kind of thinking."

HENRI NOUWEN

When I was little, I had a recurring dream. In that dream, I was on a path in the woods behind our house, walking farther away from home and deeper into the woods. I felt lost; I didn't know which way to go. The path would either diverge or become less obvious, and I would stop. Then I would wake up.

The dream has stayed with me my entire life. It wasn't scary or even very interesting. But it *was* vivid. I felt my emotions in the dream clearly. Even as I write today, I can picture that path and those woods.

I am no expert on dream analysis, but what strikes me now as an adult is that there was another alternative that didn't occur to me. When we get perspective, things can look different. Behind me, the house I grew up in is out of view, as is the yellow and green jungle gym my dad had built. I could turn around and take the wooded path back toward my home, until I reached the rusty jungle gym, and continue walking to find the green grass that we would hide Easter eggs in. Passing it, I arrive at the cement patio slab, leading to a sliding glass door that opened to my home.

In the dream I was so close. I just had to walk through the story of my everyday life to get back home. It was right there; I just needed to turn around to see it.

Finding your way home to yourself is not necessarily dramatic. Sure, it can be that, too. But more often than not, it is turning around and walking back through the story of your life. In that process, you walk through the pain, picking up and reclaiming what was discarded, even if what was discarded was yourself.

This is not something we only do once. It is something we return to again and again whenever we get lost. Pain will make us want to run. This is an understandable impulse. But the answer may not be in the unclear path in front of you. It may be in turning around to reclaim the story.

I sat with one of my best friends at a diner for breakfast this week. I was grateful for the wall on one side
of our booth and for the kind waiter who kept walking
when he saw my tears. I had asked my friend to read
over parts of my book and meet to talk about it. She is
a brilliant therapist, and I wanted to know her thoughts
about my therapeutic advice. But more than that, I
wanted to know what she thought about me sharing my
story. I asked her, "How will it feel to write this and walk
around in the world?"

She knew most of my story, but not all of it. That's
because I don't struggle now with the same things I did
years ago, and yet I still remember the humiliation I felt
as a teen when I told others about it, in my attempts to
get help.

This time is different. There is a sense of ownership
that comes when you understand your story.[1] There is
relief in having names for your pain. In that process you
reclaim your story from the shameful narratives overlaying it. You stop dismissing your valid experiences. You
feel more alignment with yourself and your unique journey, even if it still hurts.

It is the lack of understanding that gets us lost.

It is finding understanding that leads us home.

And so my tears over breakfast felt different. Sure,
my story is vulnerable. But it is mine. I felt relief. I felt

gratitude for finding the names for my pain all those years ago. I felt an embrace of my younger self and all that she had carried. I felt found.

My friend named what I already knew but that I needed to speak. Being comfortable with your pain allows you to make room for the pain of others. Something happens when you name and embrace your own pain.

And a door opens.

There's More Room Here Now

When you make room for all of your experience, you also make room for the experiences of others. The space you create for yourself creates a welcome for others. Empathy begets empathy; compassion, compassion.[2] The more comfortable you get with the hard parts of your own story, the more comfortable you'll be with the hard parts of someone else's.

When we think about those whom we feel comfortable telling our messy stories to, it is often those who seem comfortable with their own stories. You must be able to sit with the pain in your own life in order to be able to sit with it in other people's lives. We find new tenderness toward others who have faced the same losses. It's often an unexpected gift. And it isn't limited to those experiences that mirror our own. Our hearts open and make room for stories that do not mirror our own. We no longer fear other people's pain. We no longer participate in denying it. We open our eyes to see the pain that is like, and unlike, our own. The welcome in us creates welcome for others. This shift itself can be healing. Life will have pain. It's what we do with it and with one another in it that counts. Pain can be an invitation to find healing. And if healing isn't possible, it can be an invitation to be with one another in it, refusing to look away. That togetherness itself may provide some healing. Keep making room for it. One of the ways we find ourselves and one another is in our pain. I hope you feel found. And I hope you will also help others feel found.

Keep Going

In feeling found, you will learn to trust yourself even more. As a therapist, I see the cult of personality that arises with people in the healing professions. Whether it is an author, speaker, faith leader, or a social media phenom, the focus can be on someone as a holder of special knowledge. I don't believe in that. Period. At the heart of any healing work is an increase in, and a return to, trusting yourself, not outsourcing that trust to someone else.

I often tell my clients that I am trying to "work myself out of a job," meaning if I am doing my job, the need for my presence in their process will become less important.

As they internalize the truth they are discovering, the need for my help will become less necessary. I hope that my presence in the landscape becomes smaller and smaller until it is just a speck in the distance. Instead, I hope the beauty of understanding themselves, and a reunion with themselves, fills the canvas.

I hope to work myself out of a book, too.

In the confines of this book, I have not named every pain that some of you may have experienced. But my hope is that I have helped you understand the importance of finding that name.

I don't make promises often. I have a lot of guardrails for myself around them. This is in large part because I see the devastation that broken promises create. One thing I can promise you, though:

There *is* a name for your pain.

It exists, even if you haven't found it yet. When you do find it, it will open up new ways for you to know, love, and help yourself. It won't solve hardships, but it will help you to find the language to cope with those hardships.

It is a relief to understand. Sometimes, it changes everything about how you navigate your pain. Keep going until you find more understanding. As I try to work myself out of this book, I want to leave you with a few notes for the road ahead.

A Practice and a Posture

Naming your pain shouldn't be limited to reading this book. It works best, I believe, as a life practice. You can honor the truth of your experience every day, no matter how messy. Refuse to leave yourself. Refuse to repeat the misdiagnoses or dismissals that you have encountered. Naming your pain sounds something like this: "That *did* hurt" or "I'm still sad" or "These family arguments are too destructive for me" or "It *is* a big deal" or "I'm so angry" or "I've learned why this triggers me" or "This is not okay, and it is not okay with me."

Naming your pain can feel like "living your way into a new kind of thinking," as the quote at the beginning of this chapter says. Your choice to honor your experiences changes how you interact with your life. This is different from what we are often taught to practice. It is an embodiment of self-compassion.[3]

The posture of self-compassion is bending down to yourself, like you would to a hurting child, listening rather than judging. Paying attention. Asking what hurts. It looks like walking down the hill to yourself. It looks like noticing yourself, even if you are the only one tuning in, knowing it is normal to struggle. It feels like being embraced in your need rather than being abandoned. It hurts to be human. It is unrealistic to expect anything different. We all hurt, whether we acknowledge it or not. It feels better to say it out loud. In the absence of being able to solve the human experience, an accurate understanding of our hurt can be the relief.

If You Get Lost

When you are a child, grown-ups give important instructions about what to do if you get lost. It is usually some version of: Go to the last place you know and wait. Do not venture out, wander farther away, or try to find your way alone. Return. Stay. And wait.

Wisdom says you are more likely to be found in the last place you visited. And you are less likely to be found if you frantically try, without direction, to find your way back. It is counterintuitive to wait when you feel lost. It is counterintuitive to stay when you want to go. And it is counterintuitive to return to the place where you got lost.

When you get lost as an adult, the instructions are the same. Return to the last place you remember. More specifically, return to the place where it hurts. Return to the last place you know you were aching, because that may be where you left yourself. It may also be where you find yourself. Turning back to that place may be the way you find your way home.

Who ends a book by advising you to return to what hurts? (Slowly raising my hand.) Why? Because people suffer too long without being helped. The first step to finding the help you need is attending to your pain. We all instinctively run from pain. But we rarely know what we are running from, or, for that matter, what we are running toward. When we run from pain, we are running from ourselves. When you get lost, whether it is for a moment, a day, a week, a year, return to the last place it hurt. Why? Because when we run away, we don't learn the name for the pain. And unnamed pain is much scarier than pain you understand. Remember, to know something is to name it, and to name it is the first step in attending to it.

When you get lost, ask yourself, *Where am I hurting?*

When you start there, you can begin to find your way home. Be encouraged: The distance may not be as far as it once seemed.

Your Story Is Still Being Written

What gives me hope are all the stories I have been honored to sit with. The story that comes into therapy isn't where it ends. Pain brings people in, but it doesn't have the final say.

Our brains often stop at the hard part of the story. But I have been trained to ask, *What happened next?*[4] This is not a "before and after" question. It is an invitation to be with yourself in the next part of the story. The next part of your story is your presence in it and your understanding of it. It is reclaiming it and returning to yourself.

I hope you have felt my presence with you in this book. And I hope you take your own presence with you. Pain needs an ear *and* a hand. You deserve that kind of care.

Finally, your story is still being written, still unfolding, still revealing things about your truest self. I would like to leave you with these words:

May all of you be embraced as you continue your journey.

May the pieces of your heart that were kicked off the island know true belonging.

May the places where you felt totally lost reveal a quiet path forward.

May the things you feared saying out loud find a safe place to be heard.

May things you regret be met with a loving hand of forgiveness on your shoulder.

May the rejected parts of your heart find the deep, abiding warmth of welcome.

May the grief you carried alone be shouldered by others who are traveling with you.

May the things you felt you had to hide about yourself know the relief of unfolding.

May the parts of you that felt they couldn't go on find life coursing through them.

May the truth of who you are become more deeply rooted than your fears.

May the pain you couldn't name find loving presence and understanding.

May the parts of you that felt alone in your pain be surrounded by love.

Because love reclaims what was left.

Love never leaves you alone.

Love brings you home.

May it be so for you.

With you,
Monica

ACKNOWLEDGMENTS

Each podcast listener and each newsletter and Instagram reader, thank you. We take a chance on someone when we engage with their work, and I am grateful you took the chance on me. Thank you for being on this road with me. This work is with you in mind, and for you, too. I hope you feel seen and supported through it.

Every person who has prayed for this book, me, and the future readers, thank you. Every person who cheered me on, family and friends, thank you.

More specifically, I would like to thank:

Chad, you made me feel like I had something interesting to say before anyone cared. Thank you.

Keely, thank you for believing in me. Your steady presence through this process has been such an anchor. I am so grateful for you.

Ken, you believed in my voice when hope was dim. You helped me hear it again, and I followed the sound all the way back home. Your patience and commitment to helping me birth this book are a gift I hope to repay by continuing to write. I know I am not supposed to mix metaphors, but I couldn't help myself. Thank you.

Sandra, thank you for consistently creating a safe space for me during this time and teaching me how to do that for myself.

Cha, when that opportunity rejected me, you told me, "They're too small for you." I'm glad I listened to you, and I'm always better off when I do.

Tasha, you listened patiently years ago as I read my first chapter to you, and again as I rewrote it. Your loving safety gave me courage to keep going, and still does.

Kim, you are support, love, and loyalty personified. Your consistent care is an anchor I am so grateful for during this season. Nathan, you surprised me with a toast for turning in my manuscript, and that is who you have been for me. You notice and you cheer, thank you. Thank you both for consistently supporting our family through the unexpected difficult turns of this season.

Patty, your belief in me helped me believe in myself. Thank you for helping me feel like I have something to say. I always want to know what you think. Thank you for loving me in the intricate daily details of this journey. You've been there each step of the way. You have consistently encouraged me, especially when I wanted to give up.

Acknowledgments

Katie, you love people in a way that brings out the best in them and calls everyone to their higher self. I am no exception. You are consistently safe in a way that has made me feel safer in this big world, which has helped me create. You always made me feel like what I say is important, and it has given me wings. Steve, I know you don't like compliments, so don't read this part: you're my brother, you made me feel like I could run through a wall when I wanted to give up. I feel better in the world knowing you have our backs. Thank you both for catching us when life hit hard during these months.

Becky, your friendship makes me feel less alone in the world and is a safety I count on. You are one of my North Stars. Whenever I am worried or unsure, it's you I want to talk to. This book was no exception. Thank you for believing in this book for me when I lost hope. Thank you for caring about this so much, and for me so much. You made me feel less alone and I counted on your faith when I lost mine.

Kelli and Michael, thank you for checking in, for always asking, for caring about this book. Thank you for caring about me, Mark, and our kids during all the unexpected difficult obstacles we encountered during this season. I felt it, and I still do.

David, my big brother, I love you. I always wanted to make you laugh when I was little, but I really just wanted to make you proud. I don't think I've outgrown that.

Mom, when I was little, I asked you why you wash your hands the way you do. You looked at me and reflected, "Well, why do you wash your hands the way you do?" Thank you for being my first teacher in complicating my language and perspective. Thank you for fiercely believing in me and my writing.

Papi, I remember you working for hours and hours on your projects and books. I remember the abuelo, Casimiro, writing for hours and hours at the dining room table. I get it now. I hope I made you both proud. Thank you for cheering me on and believing in me.

My children:

Lily, your wisdom has always been beyond your years, and your heart more tender than your surroundings. How lucky I am to be your mommy and hang out with you.

Ollie, you told me I can't expect you to believe in yourself if I don't believe in myself about this book. You're right, I believe in you, and I love your tender heart.

Emma, your little steps are as loud as your dad's. Your powerful singing has filled our house since you were tiny and was the background of me writing this book. You are my little sunshine.

Acknowledgments

I love you three more than these words can express. I can't believe I get to be your mom. Thank you for being patient with me during this season. The one thing I hope to get right? Loving you as well as I can.

Mark, you are gentle strength personified. Being loved by you changed my life. You are my best friend, and I always want to be where you are. Every coffee, every talk, every time you let me cry and give up, thank you. You are the inside story. Your unwavering support and belief in me made me brave. I love you.

To my God who found me in my hurt: You are my strength, my foundation, my refuge, my comfort, and my guide. I would not be here without you. All my work is a *thank-you*.

NOTES

Chapter 1: Stuck in the Wrong Story

1. International OCD Foundation, "What You Need to Know About Obsessive Compulsive Disorder." Accessed May 6, 2024. https://iocdf.org/wp-content/uploads/2014/10/What-You-Need-To-Know-About-OCD.pdf.

Chapter 2: The Wrong Diagnosis

1. Shame definition adapted from Brené Brown, *Daring Greatly: How the Courage to Be Vulnerable Transforms the Way We Live, Love, Parent, and Lead* (New York: Gotham Books, 2012), 68–69, 71.

Chapter 3: It's Not That Big a Deal—The Hurt of Dismissal

1. "Rarely if ever": "Brené Brown on Empathy," (YouTube.com, December 10, 2013). Or you can follow this link: https://www.youtube.com/watch?v=1Evwgu369Jw&t=142s.

2. The definition for gaslighting is adapted from *Merriam-Webster Dictionary* (2023), https://www.merriam-webster.com/dictionary/gaslighting.

3. "Tendency to use spiritual ideas": John Welwood, *Toward a Psychology of Awakening: Buddhism, Psychotherapy, and the Path of Personal and Spiritual Transformation* (Berkeley, CA: Shambhala, 2002), 12–13.

Chapter 4: Listen

1. To define a corrective emotional experience, see the *APA Dictionary of Psychology*, https://dictionary.apa.org/corrective-emotional-experience.

2. Analysis backing up the idea of the importance of safe relationships can be found in these works: Maurizio Benazzo and Zaya Benazzo, directors. *The Wisdom of Trauma: A Journey to the Root of Human Pain and*

the Source of Healing, with Dr. Gabor Maté. Originally published in *Science and Nonduality* (The Hive Studios, 2021). For the documentary see Thewsidomoftrauma.com (1 hr., 27 min.). Brené Brown, *Daring Greatly: How the Courage to Be Vulnerable Transforms the Way We Live, Love, Parent, and Lead* (New York: Gotham Books, 2012), 8.

3. For more on the importance of listening to your body, see Hillary L. McBride, *The Wisdom of Your Body: Finding Healing, Wholeness, and Connection Through Embodied Living* (Grand Rapids: Brazos Press, 2021), 13.

4. "Neuroscience research shows": Bessel van der Kolk, *The Body Keeps the Score: Brain, Mind, and Body in the Healing of Trauma* (New York: Penguin Books, 2015), 208.

Chapter 5: Sherlocking Your Life

1. "To name something": Marcie Alvis Walker from her newsletter, "Black Eyed Stories," and shared with permission. Her newsletter can be found at: https://blackeyedstories.substack.com/.

2. For a helpful definition of emotional regulation, see *APA Dictionary of Psychology*, https://dictionary.apa.org/emotion-regulation.

3. "Name it to tame it" Daniel J. Siegel, *The Mindful Therapist: A Clinician's Guide to Mindsight and Neural Integration* (New York: W. W. Norton, 2010), 188–189. See also the YouTube video by Dan Siegel, "Name It to Tame It" (December 8, 2024). Or you can follow this link, https://www.youtube.com/watch?v=ZcDLzppD4Jc.

4. Understanding of the structure and function of the brain attributed to these works: Daniel Siegel, *Mindsight: The New Science of Personal Transformation* (New York: Bantam Books, 2011), 15–17, 64–66. Daniel Siegel, *The Developing Mind: How Relationships and the Brain Interact to Shape Who We Are* (New York: Guilford Press, 2020, 3rd Ed.), 506.

5. Imagining a scary animal is how I was taught to teach about the brain, informed by Siegel, who uses a snake in teaching about it in his book *Mindsight*. Terry Hargrave uses a bear in teaching about it in his book with Sharon Hargrave, *5 Days to a New Self* (United States: Cenveo-Trafton, 2016).

6. The brain integrates both left and right and with the upper and lower regions; in this chapter we're focusing most on the "upstairs and downstairs" reintegration. This idea is modeled in the video "Dr. Dan

Notes

Siegel's Hand Model of the Brain," found at drdansiegel.com (August 9, 2017), https://drdansiegel.com/hand-model-of-the-brain/. Also in Daniel Siegel and Tina Payne Bryson's *The Whole-Brain Child: 12 Revolutionary Strategies to Nurture Your Child's Developing Mind* (New York: Bantam Books, 2012), 37–65.

7. The idea of brain integration is attributed to Daniel J. Siegel in his book, *The Mindful Therapist*, 228.

8. The term "window of tolerance" is attributed to Daniel Siegel, and the concepts in this chapter are supported by the following: Siegel, *The Developing Mind*, 253. Courtney Armstrong, *Rethinking Trauma Treatment: Attachment, Memory Reconsolidation, and Resilience* (New York: W. W. Norton, 2019), 52–53. Siegel, *The Mindful Therapist*, 52, 205.

9. For more on the importance of the exhale length in breathing see Emily Nagoski and Amelia Nagoski from their book, *Burnout: The Secret of Unlocking the Stress Cycle* (New York: Ballantine Books, 2020), 15.

10. For more on cyclic sighing see the following works: Hadley Leggett. "'Cyclic Sighing' Can Help Breathe Away Anxiety," scope blog.standford.edu. February 9, 2023. Or go to the link https://scopeblog.stanford.edu/2023/02/09/cyclic-sighing-can-help-breathe-away-anxiety/. Andrew Huberman, Ph.D. "Cyclic Breathing For Beginners: Guided Breathwork by Andrew Huberman" (YouTube .com, February 25, 2023), or go to the link https://www.youtube.com /watch?v=P2rg7c0EQoE.

11. The impact of physical movement on regulating emotions supported by: Siegel and Bryson, *The Whole-Brain Child*, 57–61. Nagoski and Nagoski, *Burnout*, 15.

12. Similar teaching to the training I received online regarding the self-hold by Peter Levine can be found at "Treating Trauma: 2 Ways to Help Clients Feel Safe, with Peter Levine." (YouTube.com, June 2, 2017) or by following the link https://www.youtube.com/watch?v =G7zAseaIyFA.

13. Butterfly Hug for Bilateral Stimulation was created and developed by Lucina Artigas during her work with the survivors of Hurricane Pauline in Acapulco, Mexico, 1998. It is an EMDR technique. To read more about it see the article by Luciana Artigas and Ignacio Jarero, "The Butterfly Method for Bilateral Stimulation," EMDR Foundation,

September 2014. Or go to the link https://emdrfoundation.org/toolkit /butterfly-hug.pdf.

14. The positive impact of journaling on brain integration: Siegel, *Mindsight,* 187. Siegel and Bryson, *The Whole-Brain Child*, 14–36.

15. Our first instinct is to reach out to a safe person as described by Hillary L. McBride in her book, *The Wisdom of Your Body: Finding Healing, Wholeness, and Connection Through Embodied Living* (Grand Rapids: Brazos Press, 2021), 60–61.

Chapter 6: Redrawing Your Inner Map

1. You were shaped by necessity: Bessel A. van der Kolk, *The Body Keeps the Score: Brain, Mind, and Body in the Healing of Trauma* (United Kingdom: Penguin Publishing Group, 2015), 117.

2. "Children have a biological instinct": van der Kolk, *The Body Keeps the Score,* 117.

3. "Life narrative": Daniel J. Siegel, *Mindsight: The New Science of Personal Transformation* (New York: Bantam Books, 2011), 171.

4. "Tend to acknowledge both": Siegel, *Mindsight,* 172.

5. "Having difficult experiences": Siegel, *Mindsight,* 172–173.

6. Questions I ask in therapy sessions referenced in this chapter are based on the "Adult Attachment Interview" by C. George, M. Main, and N. Kaplan (1985). Adult attachment interview [Dataset]. In PsycTESTS Dataset, https://doi.org/10.1037/t02879-000.

7. Attachment styles and their impact on our development in families: Daniel J. Siegel and Mary Hartzell, *Parenting from the Inside Out: How a Deeper Self-Understanding Can Help You Raise Children Who Thrive: 10th Anniversary Edition* (United States: Penguin Publishing Group, 2013), 134–136. Robert Karen, *Becoming Attached: First Relationships and How They Shape Our Capacity to Love* (United Kingdom: Oxford University Press, 1998).

8. The concept of children as egocentric by nature is attributed to Jean Piaget and his stages of cognitive development.

Chapter 7: What Did They Call You?

1. The definition for *hook* is adapted from *Merriam-Webster Dictionary* (2023), https://www.merriam-webster.com/dictionary/hook.

2. The idea of "not caring what others think" being ineffective is

attributed to Brené Brown in her book, *Daring Greatly: How the Courage to Be Vulnerable Transforms the Way We Live, Love, Parent, and Lead* (New York: Gotham Books, 2012), 169.

Chapter 8: Is This Trauma?

1.   Research demonstrating trauma is more common than many think can be found in the 2023 CDC report, which states: "About 64% of U.S. adults reported they had experienced at least one type of ACE before age 18, and nearly 1 in 6 (17.3%) reported they had experienced four or more types of ACEs. These are significant traumas, and so 64% of adults have experience at least one." "Fast Facts: Preventing Adverse Childhood Experiences," June 29, 2023, https://www.cdc.gov/violenceprevention /aces/fastfact.html.

2.   For more on the symptoms of trauma see Peter Levine's book, *Healing Trauma* (Louisville, CO: Sounds True, 2008), 12–20.

3.   "When our bodies are feeling uneasy" is from Peter Levine's book, *Healing Trauma*, 14.

4.   The concept of stress and trauma on a continuum is attributed to Hillary L. McBride in her book *The Wisdom of Your Body: Finding Healing, Wholeness, and Connection Through Embodied Living* (Grand Rapids: Brazos Press, 2021), 58–59.

5.   "A stressful event becomes a trauma": McBride, *The Wisdom of Your Body*, 59.

6.   For more on the categories of trauma see Peter Levine's book, *Healing Trauma* (Louisville, CO: Sounds True, 2008), 12–13.

Big T trauma as defined by American Psychiatric Association, *Diagnostic and Statistical Manual of Mental Disorders*, 5th ed. (Washington, DC: American Psychiatric Association, 2013), 271.

7.   The concept of big T trauma and little t trauma as a knife wound versus paper cuts comes from Aundi Kolber in her book, *Try Softer: A Fresh Approach to Move Us out of Anxiety, Stress, and Survival Mode and into a Life of Connection and Joy* (Carol Stream, Illinois: Tyndale Momentum: 2020), 37–38.

8.   The concept of trauma in the brain as a wire hanger is attributed to Bruce D. Perry in his book with Oprah Winfrey, *What Happened to You?: Conversations on Trauma, Resilience, and Healing* (New York: Flat Iron Books, 2021), 190–194.

9. "Therapy is more about": Perry and Winfrey, *What Happened to You?*, 183.

Chapter 9: The Loneliness in Grief

1. "Her absence is like": C. S. Lewis, *A Grief Observed* (London: Faber & Faber, 2012), chapter 3.

2. "Learning to weep": Henry Nouwen, *Reaching Out: The Three Movements of the Spiritual Life* (New York: Image Books, 1986), 36.

3. The research showing that people are lonely is from Dr. Vivek Murthy, the Surgeon General of the United States, "New Surgeon General Advisory Raises Alarm about the Devastating Impact of the Epidemic of Loneliness and Isolation in the United States," May 3, 2023; or go to the link https://www.hhs.gov/about/news/2023/05/03/new-surgeon -general-advisory-raises-alarm-about-devastating-impact-epidemic -loneliness-isolation-united-states.html.

4. The concept of anger as a secondary emotion is taught often. I learned it in a training by emotionally focused couples therapy trainer Michael Barnett, LPC, at LifeGate Counseling Center.

5. Support for the statement that our brains register emotional pain in the same way they register physical pain can be found in Matthew D. Lieberman, *Social: Why Our Brains Are Wired to Connect* (New York: Crown, 2013). A video explanation of this by Matthew D. Lieberman can be found on YouTube: "On the surprising neuroscience of emotional pain" (Oxford University Press, November 5, 2013). Or go to the link https://www.youtube.com/watch?v=LBw0iqo5U2k.

Chapter 10: Underneath the Anxiety

1. Anxiety disorders versus everyday anxiety are described in Edmund J. Bourne's *Anxiety & Phobia Workbook*, vol. 1. (Oakland, CA: New Harbinger Publications, 2005), 8–9.

2. Research supporting the concept that unresolved trauma can create anxiety is supported by the following works: Bruce D. Perry and Oprah Winfrey, *What Happened to You?: Conversations on Trauma, Resilience, and Healing* (New York: Flat Iron Books, 2021). Bessel van der Kolk, *The Body Keeps the Score: Brain, Mind, and Body in the Healing of Trauma* (United Kingdom: Penguin Publishing Group, 2015).

3. Anxiety is described as a coping mechanism by Terry D. Hargrave

and Franz Pfitzer, *Restoration Therapy: Understanding and Guiding Healing in Marriage and Family Therapy* (New York, Routledge, 2011), 33–62.

4. "Foreboding joy" comes from the work of Brené Brown: Brené Brown, *Daring Greatly: How the Courage to Be Vulnerable Transforms the Way We Live, Love, Parent, and Lead* (New York: Gotham Books, 2012), 117–122, 123–127. Brené Brown's TED Talk, "The Price of Invulnerability: Brené Brown at TEDxKC" (YouTube.com. October 12, 2010); or go to the link https://www.youtube.com/watch?v=_UoMXF73j0c.

5. The concept that anxious people tend to underestimate themselves and overestimate what they are facing can be found in this article by Judith S. Beck and Robert Hindman, "Coping with Anxiety," Beck Institute, August, 2021. Or go to the link https://beckinstitute.org/wp-content/uploads/2021/08/Coping-with-Anxiety.pdf.

6. For more on anxiety in the body see the following works: Van der Kolk, *The Body Keeps the Score*. Stephen W. Porges, *The Pocket Guide to the Polyvagal Theory: The Transformative Power of Feeling Safe* (United Kingdom: W. W. Norton, 2017). Hillary L. McBride, *The Wisdom of Your Body: Finding Healing, Wholeness, and Connection Through Embodied Living* (Grand Rapids: Brazos Press, 2021).

7. The concept of anxiety as an "alarm" in the body has been attributed to different sources. Many cite Dr. David Barlow as the first person to use the term "alarm" for anxiety in the body. The author first heard this terminology used by Dr. Russel Kennedy (author of *Anxiety Rx: A New Prescription for Anxiety Relief from the Doctor Who Created It*) on a podcast episode.

Chapter 11: The Painful "Why" of Boundary Issues

1. Definition of boundaries and metaphor of yard adapted from Dr. Henry Cloud and Dr. John Townsend, *Boundaries: When to Say Yes, How to Say No, to Take Control of Your Life* (Grand Rapids: Zondervan, 1992, 2017).

2. Resentment as defined by Brené Brown in *Atlas of the Heart: Mapping Meaningful Connection and the Language of Human Experience* (United States: Random House Publishing Group, 2021), 33.

3. The term "emotional safety" has been attributed to Don R. Catherall, who created a couples therapy approach based on emotional safety.

Don. R. Catherall, *Emotional Safety: Viewing Couples Through the Lens of Affect* (New York: Routledge, 2007).

4. More on polyvagal theory referenced in this chapter can be found here: Stephen W. Porges, *The Polyvagal Theory: Neurophysiological Foundations of Emotions, Attachment, Communication, Self-Regulation* (United Kingdom: W. W. Norton, 2011). Stephen W. Porges, *The Pocket Guide to the Polyvagal Theory: The Transformative Power of Feeling Safe* (United Kingdom: W. W. Norton, 2017).

5. Pete Walker, *Complex PTSD: From Surviving to Thriving* (Lafayette, CA: Azure Coyote Publishing, 2013).

6. "Fawn types": Pete Walker, "The 4Fs: A Trauma Typology in Complex PTSD," https://pete-walker.com/fourFs_TraumaTypology ComplexPTSD.htm, April 28, 2024.

7. Definition of secure attachment and the freedom to share negative emotions in those relationships are described by Robert Karen, *Becoming Attached: First Relationships and How They Shape Our Capacity to Love* (United Kingdom: Oxford University Press, 1998), 6, 241–242.

Chapter 12: This Is Too Much

1. Shootings referenced in this chapter can be found at the following links: https://www.cnn.com/2023/08/29/us/unc-chapel-hill-campus-shooting-tuesday/index.html; https://www.pbs.org/newshour/nation/jacksonville-shooter-who-killed-3-used-to-work-at-a-dollar-store.

2. My therapeutic lens for loving yourself is informed by the work on self-compassion by Dr. Kristin Neff in her book *Self-Compassion: The Proven Power of Being Kind to Yourself* (Kingdom: HarperCollins, 2011).

3. Richard Rohr, *A Spring Within Us: A Book of Daily Meditations* (CAC Publishing: 2016), 199, 120–121.

4. Support for the idea that compassion for oneself increases your compassion with others: Laura R. Welp and Christina M. Brown, "Self-compassion, Empathy, and Helping Intentions," *The Journal of Positive Psychology* 9 (2013): 54–65. Svoboda, Elizabeth. "Self-Compassion Could Help You Be More Tolerant of Others," (greatergood.berkley.edu, January 9, 2023). https://greatergood.berkeley.edu/article/item/self_compassion_could_help_you_be_more_tolerant_of_others.

Notes

Chapter 13: What Was Your Creative Strategy?

1. Research on the impact of how one defines PTSD and stress responses, as well as the concept of symptoms as "allies," is in Courtney Armstrong, *Rethinking Trauma Treatment: Attachment, Memory Reconsolidation, and Resilience* (New York: W.W. Norton & Company, 2019), 75–76.

2. "Globalize" means to make worldwide in scope or application, as cited in Merriam Webster, https://www.merriam-webster.com/dictionary /globalize.

3. Read more about how our brains remember stressful things in this article by Anne Bierbrauer, Marie-Christin Fellner, Rebekka Heinen, Oliver T. Wolf, and Nikolai Axmacher, "The Memory Trace of a Stressful Episode," *Current Biology*. Published online October 2021, https:// www.x-mol.net/paper/article/1448739391137546240.

4. Therapeutic conceptualization of coping as a response to messages about safety and identity adapted from Terry D. Hargrave and Franz Pfitzer, *Restoration Therapy: Understanding and Guiding Healing in Marriage and Family Therapy* (New York: Routledge, 2011), 3–31.

5. Coping styles adapted and shared with permission from the book by Terry Hargrave and Sharon Hargrave, *5 Days to a New Self* (United States: Cenveo-Trafton, 2016).

6. You can see it on this scene from *Moana* on YouTube by searching: Moana, "Know Who You Are" (3:39) or by following this link: https:// youtu.be/BZ9OR_S1OXw?si=x2ZemFIQMwNvO3o7.

Chapter 14: What's the Story You've Been Believing?

1. "Core beliefs" are a concept credited to Aaron T. Beck, the founder of Cognitive-Behavioral Therapy. For more on core beliefs determining feelings about who you are: Zawn Villines, "Core Beliefs: What They Are and How to Identify Them," Medicalnewstoday.com, February 23, 2023; or go to the link https://www.medicalnewstoday.com/articles/core-beliefs. F. Osmo, et al. "The Negative Core Beliefs Inventory: Development and Psychometric Properties," *Journal of Cognitive Psychotherapy* 32, no. 1, April 2018. Or go to the link https://connect.springerpub.com/content /sgrjcp/32/1/67.

Notes

2. Core beliefs are also referred to as "silent assumptions," as described by David D. Burns, *Feeling Good: The New Mood Therapy* (United Kingdom: HarperCollins, 2008).

3. Our feeling about identity and safety adapted from restoration therapy, shared with permission from Hargrave and Hargrave, *5 Days to a New Self* (United States: Cenveo-Trafton, 2016) as well as Terry D. Hargrave and Franz Pfitzer, *Restoration Therapy: Understanding and Guiding Healing in Marriage and Family Therapy* (New York: Routledge, 2011), 3–31.

4. The limbic area of the brain is often asking: "Is this good or bad?" "Am I safe?": Daniel J. Siegel, "Dr. Dan Siegel's Hand Model of the Brain," drdansiegel.com, August 9, 2017. Or go to the link https://drdansiegel.com/hand-model-of-the-brain/. Daniel J. Siegel, *Mindsight: The New Science of Personal Transformation* (New York: Bantam Books, 2011), 15. Daniel J. Siegel and Tina Payne Bryson, *The Whole-Brain Child: 12 Revolutionary Strategies to Nurture Your Child's Developing Mind* (New York: Bantam Books, 2012), 37–65.

Chapter 15: You Are Not Your Pain

1. When I refer to feeling the weight of emotional pain in your body, this idea is influenced by the research of Bessel van der Kolk in *The Body Keeps the Score: Brain, Mind, and Body in the Healing of Trauma* (United Kingdom: Penguin Publishing Group, 2015).

2. My therapeutic lens of our "younger selves" is influenced by the following works: Peter A. Levine and Ann Frederick, *Waking the Tiger: Healing Trauma: The Innate Capacity to Transform Overwhelming Experiences* (Berkeley, CA: North Atlantic Books, 1997). Richard C. Schwartz, *No Bad Parts: Healing Trauma and Restoring Wholeness with the Internal Family Systems Model* (Louisville, CO: Sounds True, 2021). Robert Karen, *Becoming Attached: First Relationships and How They Shape Our Capacity to Love* (United Kingdom: Oxford University Press, 1998).

3. Resiliency as defined here: "Resilience," Center on the Developing Child, Harvard University, Developingchildharvard.edu. Accessed September 25, 2023. Or go to the link https://developingchild.harvard.edu/science/key-concepts/resilience/. "Resilience," APA Dictionary of Psychology. Accessed September 25, 2023. Or go to the link https://www.apa.org/topics/resilience.

4. My understanding of a true self is informed by the following works:

Notes

Schwartz, *No Bad Parts*. Richard Rohr, *True Self/False Self* (Franciscan Media 2019).

5. The therapeutic intervention of "Who are you on your best day?" is attributed to Dr. Terry Hargrave, at a Restoration Therapy Training.

6. Grounding truths, adapted from Hargrave and Hargrave with permission from *5 Days to a New Self* (United States: Cenveo-Trafton, 2016), 59.

7. Research supporting neuroplasticity, and how our brains change, can be found in the following works: Matt Puderbaugh and Prabhu D. Emmady, "Neuroplasticity," StatPearls, StatPearls Publishing, May 1, 2023. Daniel J. Siegel, *Mindsight: The New Science of Personal Transformation.* (United Kingdom: Random House Publishing Group, 2010), 5, 84. Daniel J. Siegel, *The Developing Mind, Second Edition: How Relationships and the Brain Interact to Shape Who We Are* (United Kingdom: Guilford Publications, 2015), 221.

8. "Rainbow," by Kasey Musgraves, Shane McAnally, Natalie Hemby (Golden Hour, 2019).

Chapter 16: Notes for the Road

1. My therapeutic lens for owning your story is shaped by Brené Brown, *The Gifts of Imperfection: Let Go of Who You Think You're Supposed to Be and Embrace Who You Are* (New York: Simon & Schuster, 2022), as well as her book *Daring Greatly: How the Courage to Be Vulnerable Transforms the Way We Live, Love, Parent, and Lead* (New York: Avery, 2012).

2. Support for the concept that empathy begets empathy and compassion builds on compassion can be found in the following places: Mark Bekoff, "Compassion Begets Compassion: Science Shows This to Be True and We Knew It All the Time," *Psychology Today*, psychologytoday.com, July 19, 2012. David DeSteno, "Compassion Made Easy," *New York Times*, July 14, 2012. Or go to the link https://www.nytimes.com/2012/07/15/opinion/sunday/the-science-of-compassion.html?_r=1. Laura R. Welp and Christina M. Brown, "Self-Compassion, Empathy, and Helping Intentions," *Journal of Positive Psychology* 9 (2013): 13. Elizabeth Svoboda, "Self-Compassion Could Help You Be More Tolerant of Others," (greatergood.berkley.edu, January 9, 2023). https://greatergood.berkeley.edu/article/item/self_compassion_could_help_you_be_more_tolerant_of_others.

Notes

3. My definition of self-compassion is informed by Dr. Kristin Neff's work on self-compassion in her book *Self-Compassion: The Proven Power of Being Kind to Yourself* (United Kingdom: HarperCollins, 2011).

4. I was trained as a therapist to understand how your brain stops at the hard part, and to ask, "What happened next?" in the training "Creating Post-Traumatic Growth: Strategies for Resilience," November 1, 2019, conducted by Courtney Armstrong, LPC/MHSP, in Atlanta, GA. Armstrong also explores this more in her book *Rethinking Trauma Treatment: Attachment, Memory Reconsolidation, and Resilience* (New York: W. W. Norton, 2019).

ABOUT THE AUTHOR

Monica DiCristina has been a practicing therapist in Atlanta, Georgia, for more than fifteen years. She is also a sought-after speaker, podcaster, and writer on topics of emotional healing and mental health. Combining her extensive therapeutic knowledge with creativity, empathy, storytelling, and faith, she is passionate about walking alongside those who are unraveling their difficult experiences and providing a path for them to do the brave and sacred work of transformation and healing.

Monica understands the audible sigh of relief that comes when finally understanding our pain. As a child and young adult, she struggled to find a name for her mental health struggles until a caring therapist gave her the guidance she needed. Today, her heartfelt mission is to help bring the same relief to others, and educate and empower readers to do the same for themselves.

Monica is happily married to her best friend with whom she shares three children and two adorable but mischievous dogs.